Praise for *The Meaning of Geese*

Goose-nerd Nick Acheson opens his wildlife diary to us, sharing the highs and lows of a unique winter spent in nature's embrace on the windswept North Norfolk coast. *The Meaning of Geese* is an intimate study of the intriguing lives of these under-appreciated birds, as well as a window into the inner workings of a naturalist's obsession.

LEE SCHOFIELD, author of *Wild Fell*

Combining old-school charm with 2020s urgency, Nick's book, like its subject, is simultaneously earthing and elevating, evoking the bittersweet ache of belonging to a place that is changing but still and always home. The writing is measured, erudite, unfailingly generous but with an underlying emotional vibrancy that cuts through like an icy wind or the sudden dazzle of winter sun.

AMY-JANE BEER, author of *The Flow*

A fascinating and thought-provoking record of an individual and his passion for geese, among other birds. Beautifully descriptive but also detailed in the history of winged visitors to the North Norfolk coast, Nick communicates pure passion and unconditional love for a landscape that is his home. A book about geese, people, their observations and a landscape steeped in natural history.

JAKE FIENNES, author of *Land Healer*

What Nick has achieved with *The Meaning of Geese* is not just a timely, poignant meditation on his relationship with these birds and his home, but through powerful, lyrical prose, he seems to happen upon unlocking the meaning of life itself: a passionate, purposeful existence which is entirely bound to and entwined with the natural world. Relaxing yet rousing. Honest, human and heart-grabbing. I loved this book so much.

SOPHIE PAVELLE, author of *Forget Me Not*

Nick Acheson lives his life as he writes his books – full of clarity and passion. Only a man hefted so deeply to a landscape could bring the detail of wildlife to the page in such brightness. So much so that you feel you are riding on his handlebars as he toils up Norfolk's hills on his old bike in search of his beloved geese or shivering at his side as an easterly wind buffets the flocks that fuss and shout all around.

Migrant geese bring with them the spectacle of the sunlit months of northern reaches, places like Iceland, Siberia, even Canada. As the days shorten, they are guided by the stars to whiffle and glide onto the mud of the North Norfolk coast, bringing in their wake a yearning evoked by meeting travellers who have seen what we never will. But for Nick, the geese are far more than natural wonders, they are the embodiment of a rich human history, the stuff of folktales, the creatures that bind nature-loving friends together, a consolation in the dark months, and they are feathered portents of a changing planet. *The Meaning of Geese* is exactly the right title.

The details of Norfolk's wildlife, large and small, fall out of the page. As I read this book while winter nudges away the last warm days of the year, I am fired by a love for a world that still has geese sailing through the night to land amongst us and am grateful to those who wait for them to arrive and watch them with wonder.

MARY COLWELL, author of *Curlew Moon*

In *The Meaning of Geese*, Nick invites you into the realm of gaggles, honks and cackles. His gentle, warm love for all things goose shines from every page. In winter walks gone by, I might have overlooked a field full of these feathered beings, but Nick's ability to shine a spotlight of adoration, wonder and curiosity onto something right under your nose is quite wonderful. Growing up in Lancashire, a sky brimming with honking pink-footed geese is a visceral childhood memory, and I feel like Nick's goose winter has reconnected me with those feelings of awe and joy.

LUCY HODSON, naturalist and wildlife communicator

This book is an absolute treasure. Nick's attention to detail is astonishing, but he also writes with humour, humility and grace, seamlessly blending a lifetime of knowledge, insight and passion – not only for his beloved geese but for the entire natural world. I will never again look at geese without pondering their 'meaning'.

Brigit Strawbridge Howard,
author of *Dancing with Bees*

The Meaning of Geese shows us it is possible and necessary to know ourselves and our wild world through a deep intimacy with just one place under the sky – and the simple reach of a mother's happy red-darter-coloured bicycle. In an awe-filled and absorbing portrait, wild geese bring the world and its mysteries to us and our shared landscape.

The warmth, humility, friendship and deep knowledge that exude from this book are infectious and necessary. It is a lyrical love letter to North Norfolk, its skies, people and the gleaming, binding, gossamer threads its geese trail across the globe and back. *The Meaning of Geese* shows us how we too can be explorers and pioneers of a deeper knowledge, from the seat of an old red bicycle.

Nicola Chester, author of *On Gallows Down*

A delightful account of a low-tech (and low-carbon) quest to follow, watch and understand one of Britain's greatest bird spectacles: the huge flocks of pink-footed geese that visit our shores from the far north each autumn and winter.

Stephen Moss, author of
Ten Birds that Changed the World

THE MEANING OF GEESE

THE MEANING OF GEESE

A thousand miles
in search of home

NICK ACHESON

Chelsea Green Publishing
White River Junction, Vermont
London, UK

*For my parents, my siblings and their families,
my first and forever flock.*

Copyright © 2023 by Nick Acheson.

All rights reserved.

No part of this book may be transmitted or reproduced in any form by any means without permission in writing from the publisher.

Commissioning Editor: Muna Reyal
Project Manager: Angela Boyle
Copy Editor: Susan Pegg
Proofreader: Nikki Sinclair
Designer: Melissa Jacobson

Printed in the United Kingdom.
First printing January 2023.
10 9 8 7 6 5 4 3 2 1   23 24 25 26 27

ISBN 978-1-91529-409-8 (hardcover)
ISBN 978-1-91529-410-4 (ebook)
ISBN 978-1-91529-411-1 (audiobook)

Chelsea Green Publishing
85 North Main Street, Suite 120
White River Junction, Vermont USA

Somerset House
London, UK

www.chelseagreen.co.uk

CONTENTS

PROLOGUE: ...an edgeless place,
of land and sea and sky — 1

2020

SEPTEMBER: summer dies slowly — 11
OCTOBER: a thousand pinks — 27
NOVEMBER: wild, empty spaces — 61
DECEMBER: a heaving mass
of blue-grey backs — 97

2021

JANUARY: what tales of Arctic tundras
or of temperate lakes — 131
FEBRUARY: a cycling milestone — 165
MARCH: decisions with
unintended consequences — 185
APRIL: the final stanza in this
song of geese — 201

EPILOGUE — 217

Wild Geese, Their People and
Their Places in Norfolk — 221
Acknowledgements — 225
Bibliography — 227

PROLOGUE

…an edgeless place, of land and sea and sky

The coast of Norfolk is an edgeless place, of land and sea and sky all seeping into one another. It is a place of change, exchange, fluidity, where sediments, water, genes and carbon are all cycled and recycled endlessly. And it is my home.

The Wash is coastal Norfolk's western outpost, a missing notch from England's eastern flank which has been filled, by rivers and the tide, with silt. Twice a day the moon turns mud to sea here. Twice a day a billion animals' lives are radically altered. Under the briny tide, countless cockles harvest plankton and innumerable other invertebrates feed. A second tide – of birds – occurs now too: tens and sometimes hundreds of thousands of wading birds driven from the muddy, food-rich safety of the Wash onto forbidding land. By its very nature, the Wash is all exchange.

Our saltmarshes, stretching from Holme to Kelling, and echoed around Breydon Water in the east, are just as obviously fluid as the Wash: subject to daily tides and yearly storms and migrant flows of wigeon, curlews, brent geese. The sand dunes, grazing marsh and shingle of North

The Meaning of Geese

Norfolk's coast seem, by contrast, constant, but their fluidity is merely measured over greater time. They too are children of the ever-changing wind and waves. They too are flux.

Our dunes are made by wind, whipping sand inland until it falters and is colonised by prickly saltwort and sea rocket. Sand couch comes next, pinning the mobile sand in place, crafting the conditions required by marram, which will build and stabilise the dune. Where there is shingle on our coast, as at Cley and Salthouse, it has been hurled ashore by waves. Then, over time, it has been softened by the kindly touch of common cat's-ear, sea campion and biting stonecrop. Though seeming stable, these coastal habitats are always changing too. Thrashed by November storms, they are scoured away or violently pushed inland. The stop-start process of their formation begins again.

East of this low, north-facing stretch of sand and shingle, sea and sky, is Norfolk's northeast shoulder. Reaching from Weybourne down to Happisburgh, this is a coast of cliffs. On a bed of chalk – the graveyard of untold trillions of Late Cretaceous phytoplankton – sits a layer of mud. Three quarters of a million years in age, this is the silty, sludgy bottom of a limitless estuary. Within it are the bones of hippos, rhinos, elephants, shrews and sticklebacks. Above this mud – mere infants in geological time – stand cliffs of sand and rubble pushed here beneath the crawling bellies of late Pleistocene ice sheets. Unlike the staunch, resistant schists and granites of the UK's west and northern coasts, our Norfolk cliffs are soft and vulnerable. Weighed down by rain, they slump onto the beach, where their sand and clay are gnawed by unrelenting waves and tide. Here the land is slowly – sometimes dramatically – giving way to sea and sky again.

Still further south, where Norfolk faces east, just before becoming Suffolk, lie the Broads. This is a low, coalescent

Prologue

landscape, where saltwater, freshwater, soil and sky all blend. As recently as Roman times, much of what we know today as Broadland was subject to the tide, and it is likely that – with our changing climate – much of the land will soon surrender to the tide again. For now, embraced only by a flimsy bar of coastal dunes, this is an untamed waterscape of reed and fen, of barely anchored wetland woods and Mediaeval pits dug out for peat.

Both along our low north stretch of coast and in the Broads, there's grazing marsh. Uniquely, this is habitat shaped by people. Where they are found along North Norfolk's coast – at Holme, at Holkham and at Cley – grazing marshes have been stolen from the sea. Historically, more money could be made from grazing sheep and cattle on grassland fed by springs in Norfolk's underlying chalk than could be made on saltmarsh. From the seventeenth century, wealthy landowners had saltmarshes embanked, keeping out the timeless tide and banishing salt. These obdurate, sea-resisting walls jar with our shifting, edgeless coast, where sea and land and sky are one. But, with the North Sea hungering to breach them, their time is almost done.

It was in grazing marsh that my life with Norfolk's geese began. On any given Saturday in November and December 1987, a big white van – a black kite stencilled on its driver's door – was parked along Cley Beach Road in North Norfolk. The driver was a biology teacher from a nearby school, with a patient passion for sharing natural history with his pupils. The four boys huddled in the back, clutching beginner binoculars, had all been taken beneath his wing.

One of the boys, in cheap black wellies, charcoal school trousers doing nothing to protect his scrawny legs from winter's cold, peered with bright blue eyes from under a thick brown fringe. Insecure and timid though he was, he loved these Saturday morning outings to the coast. Little though they knew it then, the boys were learning, from their kind, red-spectacled teacher, a way of looking on the world. Their lives were being peopled with wild friends, whose arrivals and departures would forever mark their seasons.

In November 1987, beside Beach Road, the teacher and the boys were watching geese. Though doubtless a few feral Canada geese were nearby too, our focus – for I'm the mop-haired boy, of course – was on a flock of brent geese, hundreds strong: dark-bellied brent geese from Siberia, Norfolk's salt-marsh geese. In the memory of my slight boy self, the winter Eye Field – embanked as grazing marsh from the 1600s – was always gloomy but also always full of brents, the cold air resonant with their throaty murmur. Here our teacher – still among my dearest friends today – taught us to distinguish the year's youngsters by their neat, white-pencilled backs; taught us to look for families in the flocks; taught us about their cycles of success, mirroring booms in lemmings on the tundra. With his guidance, brents were the first geese that I learned to love.

The binoculars that I had back then were dreadful but it mattered nothing. Each time I raised their icy metal to my face, to watch these wondrous beings, I was conveyed into their Arctic lives, into a wild where I belonged. Among Siberian geese and birdwatchers, I'd found my flock.

From December 1987, a lone red-breasted goose was with the brents at Cley. I knew red-breasted geese because a captive pair lived in the next-door garden to the farmhouse where I grew up. On summer evenings I would lie in bed, the buckled sash window of my bedroom open, listening to the disyllabic squeak of these exquisite birds, imagining their species' distant life on the fox-haunted tundra of west Siberia.

Prologue

All through my first goose winter at Cley, until March when it migrated, I longed to see this lost Siberian jewel. Somehow, though all my new friends saw it, I was never there when it appeared. It would be many years until a redbreast joined the winter flock of brents a few miles west at Wells and finally I saw a bird I'd dreamed of since I'd thumbed my mother's copy of Peter Scott's key to waterfowl as a child.

The brents though, I saw them every week, and have loved them ever since. Their burbling voices are the soul of Norfolk's winter saltmarsh. Their stubby legs and tubby bellies are midwinter constants in cereal fields across North Norfolk. But they were not the only geese I learned to love that winter. This was a time of pinkfeet too. For more than thirty winters, Iceland's pink-footed geese had been missing from ancestral roosts at Wells and Holkham, until the early 1980s when they started to return. Sometimes our teacher would cast the net of our adventures wider, visiting places further afield, including Holkham and its pinkfeet, in the west.

With reverence in our voices, we watched these first returning pinkfeet, marvelling that they had come again. Unlike Cley's confiding brents – boldly marked in black and white and graphite – Holkham's pinkfeet were shy and indefinable, their pastel greys and blues and fawns bleeding into one another, like coastal Norfolk's sea and soil and sky. Not so their fierce, insistent voices, carrying with them all the summer drama of Icelandic uplands, thrilling us with wildness every time we heard them.

Through our school and university years, we boys remained firm friends and grew to know and love more winter geese. Brents and pinkfeet are the core geese of a Norfolk winter, but the Holkham grazing marsh was also visited by a handsome flock of Russian white-fronted geese, as it still is to this day. These are slim-necked, mid-grey geese, with neat pink bills and orange legs; their striking foreheads white, their bellies heavily blotched and barred in black.

Last of the winter geese we tried to see each year – most enigmatic too – the taiga bean goose is an elegant bird from boreal forests of Scandinavia and Russia, with just two winter flocks in the UK. Faithful to their winter feeding grounds, one flock visits the Slamannan Plateau south of Falkirk every year. The other, which numbered in the hundreds in my childhood but has dwindled almost to disappearance now, visits the marshes of the River Yare, southeast of Norwich. Once a year, we would make the journey to the Broads, and we would stand above the River Yare, our telescopes trained on distant rushy grassland, searching for the long-necked silhouettes of these elusive geese.

Wild geese were simply always there, the sound and spectacle of my winters. As much a part of Norfolk's edgeless coast as sand and shingle, they called me home from university to my flock, both bird and human. But somehow, during my MSc, adrift and low, I moved to Bolivia, which for ten years became my home.

There was noise here too, of course: the riotous jabbering of chachalacas and the rolling storms of howler monkey families. The chiming shrieks of seriemas filled savannahs and, deep in the forest, the jaguar gave its moaning roar. Just as along my Norfolk coast, there was flux and flow here too. Great rivers of Amazonia – puffing with river dolphins – carried unimaginable quantities of water, silt and logs. Along them there were shifting bars and islands, on which large-billed terns and collared plovers nested; in whose sun-baked sands side-necked turtles dug to lay their eggs. I was so enraptured by it all that geese slipped into the background of my mind.

Prologue

While working for a conservation charity, I was asked to lead a group of donors from the United States, as they visited a protected area in the remote northeast, which they helped to fund. This was a peerless park, where Amazonia met the ancient Brazilian Shield and where Bolivia met Brazil. Here, lowland tapirs bathed in spiny palm swamps, the black stilt legs of maned wolves and the great brush tails of giant anteaters swayed across savannahs, and hoatzins coughed from every riverside tree. The trip was a success and I was asked to lead again.

Before I knew it, I was leading birdwatching tours all over Bolivia, watching red-fronted macaws in the country's unique dry Andean valleys and calling golden-headed quetzals from humid forests with whistled imitations of their songs. It was a time of magic.

I rarely visited England – on the wages of Bolivian conservation charities, I could ill afford to – but after ten years, at a forked path in my life, I was home at Christmas, wondering whether my days in South America were done. A friend invited me for a walk. We met at Stiffkey and ambled east along the seawall towards Morston, saltmarsh to the left of us and grazing marsh to the right. The air was bright with the winter whistles of wigeon; but what I recall most clearly was a flock of brent geese feeding in the grazing marsh, less than a hundred metres from us.

My binoculars were in Bolivia, a sayaca tanager no doubt singing in the palm beside the window where they lay. My old friend handed me his pair, so I could watch the brents. Binoculars are cushioned in rubber armour now, no longer metallic and cold, but, as I raised them to my face, I became a boy again. Five years at university, ten years of hyacinth macaws and Andean flamingos, slipped away. On a cold, bright day by a Norfolk grazing marsh, I was with my flock.

The Meaning of Geese

With my friend's binoculars I quickly found a rarer goose. Almost all the birds – fifty perhaps – were dark-bellied brent geese, our regular winter visitors from west Siberia. Among them there was one black brant, from the distant tundra of the North Pacific. Blacker on the back and belly than the rest, with a bolder white collar and a broad white flank, this dapper goose was in the flock but somehow other.

For ten years, in South America, I'd been the foreigner in the flock: accepted, loved, but always other. Seeing this goose, I knew it was time to return to Norfolk, to my home. A little further on, though I'd said nothing, my friend brought up a seasonal job on offer in his department at the conservation charity where he worked. Almost disbelieving, I asked whether – with all my experience in the wrong landscapes, on the wrong side of the world – there was any chance that I would get it if I applied.

I got the job, though for propriety my friend stood down from interviewing. I moved home from Bolivia. A few weeks later, hearing my first returning willow warbler in a decade, in the village where I grew up, I sobbed. Wave after wave of sobbing moved across me, like rain in summer storms. In the soulful, liquid voice of this continent-defying little bird, came the knowing that I was home.

By now, though, I was well known for leading wildlife tours. Offers kept coming to work in ever wilder and more thrilling places. Over the next ten years, around jobs in conservation at home, I worked on every continent, on every ocean, sharing wildlife with my clients and learning from brilliant, passionate colleagues everywhere. It was a life of enormous privilege.

And guilt. It was during these years that the scale of our environmental crisis became apparent. The more I read and thought, the more I hated flying. The more I hated myself

Prologue

for flying. I'd got into a position in which the majority of my income came from leading extraordinary wildlife tours; in which friends across the world asked me to keep supporting both their businesses and their conservation projects; in which clients' and colleagues' lives were genuinely changed by the experiences we shared. It took deep thought and anguish for me to decide I had to give up flying; for me to tell the tour company I worked for, and my many friends there, how I felt.

In November 2019, I came home from Sichuan, from watching Pallas's cat, Chinese mountain cat, Chinese red panda, golden snub-nosed monkey and Lady Amherst's pheasant. With that, my travel commitments were all but done. Then, early in 2020, our whole world changed. Just as the Ice Age cliffs of Norfolk can seem eternal, until a catastrophic mudslide devours a hundred-metre stretch, so we were thrust into a life we neither recognised nor understood.

Like innumerable others, for the first two months I was alone. Even once the rules relaxed, I remained alone, thanks to ill health among my closest family. Just as alarmingly, I soon had essentially no income. Despite this, spring and summer, with their blissful weather, and no vehicles on the roads, were a time of happiness for me. I walked and watched and wondered at the wildlife on my doorstep. Ten species of warbler sang upriver from my home, as every year they do; a badger trotted past my door as I left to walk one early morning; ring ouzels poured through my stretch of valley in numbers nobody had ever seen; a corncrake from the Norfolk reintroduction settled in an ancient meadow by my house; and a white-tailed eagle from the Isle of Wight flew over as I drank black coffee in my garden.

But I'm not good at winter. As robins began to sing in autumn, presaging in their tragic songs the cold and lonely

The Meaning of Geese

months ahead, I became low. I had no work still. Still I was alone. Unable to flock with those I loved, I decided I would join another flock, the one which brought me home from South America. I would follow Norfolk's geese all winter, I would write about them, and about the many people whose lives they touched. Both to keep my emissions low and, in my tiny way, to honour the great, athletic migrations of our geese, I would dust off my mother's old red bike and cycle.

I wrote to two friends whose knowledge of geese is legendary. One of them, Andy Bloomfield, is senior warden of the Holkham National Nature Reserve. Born at Holkham, he knows its wildlife as no one else, including winter's brents and whitefronts, and the pinkfeet which he has watched since their return in the 1980s. The second, Kane Brides, works for the Wildfowl and Wetlands Trust. He has ringed and studied geese all over Europe, especially in Iceland, where our pinkfeet breed. Both friends replied with enthusiasm and agreed to help.

September came and swallows gathered above the village duckpond by my house. The swifts had left already, leaving a screaming silence in their stead. But my phone whirred with news of pink-footed geese crossing the Hebrides, coming south. On 6th September Andy texted that 300 pinks had come to roost at Holkham, the first arrivals of the year. The following morning, I fetched my red bike from the shed and cycled twelve miles to the coast, and Holkham. With this, I launched into a winter to be spent with Norfolk's brents and pinkfeet; with the geese which, thirty years before, a scrawny, mop-haired boy had learned to love.

2020

SEPTEMBER

summer dies slowly

Pink-footed geese arrive from Iceland. Cycling around North Norfolk on my old red bike, I find them feeding in coastal stubble fields. By the month's end, as the weather grows cold, the first dark-bellied brent geese arrive from Siberia.

Monday 7th September

Summer dies slowly, in dark bush-crickets' muted chirps and in the bead-eyed common gulls drawn from northern moors to Norfolk's plough. Winter comes slowly too, in the gathering of the geese. I saw my first today. Pink-footed geese of course – for they come first – and they're early this year again. They came into my mind some weeks ago, as their numbers swelled in the south of Iceland and I began to conceive a season writing words on geese. I primed goose-expert friends, and for the past two days the phone in my pocket has buzzed with news of their noisy flocks over the Hebrides and Highlands. Last night, newly arrived, 300 pinkfeet came to roost at Holkham, close to my North Norfolk home.

I went to welcome them this morning. Reaching the end of Lady Anne's Drive, and Holkham's coastal grazing marsh, I heard, through a North Sea fret, the shrill Norse gossip of

The Meaning of Geese

the geese, somewhere overhead. Here again; home again in Norfolk. Between the pine crowns on the dunes, and through the mist, I caught the subtly readjusting V that presages a Norfolk winter, still more felt than seen. At Salts Hole, 500 metres further west, four pinkfeet dropped from the mucky sky to the grazing marsh beyond, tilting their blue-grey wings to stall, and fall to our sun-sweet southern grass.

Four geese: parents with their tundra-born goslings of this year. Two young which, still eggs barely three months ago, have made a maiden journey south, to come to Holkham. They will stay together here, this family, all winter, and across the muddy fields of North Norfolk and the Broads. In early spring – hunger, foxes and the gun permitting – they will start to make their way together to the tundra. I will stay with them throughout the winter too, and write a story of geese and of people and the land.

I walked a little further to the west, stopping to lean on the crumbling wall above the Iceni fort. From inland of Burnham Overy, large skeins of geese appeared, twisting grey squiggles in the wet grey sky. I tingled with excitement: here they came. Their voices reached me, though, before a hint of plumage: the nasal clang that said their bills were deep-based and orange, not delicate and tipped with pink. Greylags are fine geese nonetheless – unfairly scorned – and they will feature in this story too. I tingled still as they reached the marsh and tumbled, hurling their silver-shouldered wings from side to side, and landed on a pool fringed in purple-headed reed, from which a Cetti's warbler damply sang, claiming his space in a distant spring.

Another voice: a high Icelandic yicker, as four more pinkfeet came to Holkham at last. They dipped to join the greylags; then, perceiving their mistake, wheeled up and on

September

to land unseen a little further. Tears filled my eyes as this sky-borne family dropped to our Norfolk mud and grass and I stood humbled by the journey they've survived, excited by a winter ahead in the company of geese.

Curlews called balefully across the marsh, and meadow pipits lisped over the pines, bound south too. Even the rolled Rs of house martins sounded sad today, through mist and drizzle; a sound so happy when they come in April. I trudged back to my bike in the rain. For I'd cycled the twelve and more miles from home in honour of the pinks, in honour of their long unbroken flight here from the Arctic Circle's southern fringe.

It was a paltry tribute to these magnificent birds. Even so, the first four miles of my journey home, from the coast at Wells to Egmere, are a long, slow hill, taxing my mother's forty-one-year-old bike, taxing my all-but-forty-seven-year-old thighs. The drizzle fell and caravans tore past, heading for home, hardly heeding a cyclist straining up a hill in honour of Icelandic geese.

I reached home wet. As I'd lain in bed before dawn, listening to Radio Four, Tomasz Schafernaker's chipper voice had promised that East Anglia's weather would be fine and dry. Last time I trust his pillow talk.

Wednesday 9th September

Geese called me to the coast again today. All yesterday, as I was working in the Brecks, news came to me of pinkfeet reaching Norfolk. Eager to see them as they arrived, I took to my bike – the colour of a ruddy darter dragonfly – and went, through a sweaty western wind, downhill to Holkham. Stretching my arm to signal I was heading northward, off the coast road to the marsh, I heard pinks yapping overhead. Twenty of them, bound inland.

In the 1860s, when Henry Stevenson was writing *The Birds of Norfolk*, the pink-footed goose had only for a matter of decades been described as a species separate from the bean goose. It had thus only recently been shown that Holkham's winter flocks of geese were pinkfeet and not beans. 'The earliest record of its identification in this county,' Stevenson writes, 'is apparently the notice by Yarrell of a specimen killed at Holkham, in January, 1841, by the present Earl of Leicester out of a flock of about twenty, since which time this goose has proved to be by far the most common species that frequents the Holkham marshes.'

Stevenson goes on to quote the Earl of Leicester, who lived at Holkham and owned the marshes which – still in his descendants' care – form part of a National Nature Reserve today. 'As long as I can recollect wild geese frequented the Holkham and Burnham Marshes. Their time of appearing in this district is generally the last week of October, and their departure the end of March, varying a little according to the season.'

To a watcher of geese in modern Norfolk, it is remarkable that in the 1800s pink-footed geese did not reach Holkham until the last week of October, which at the time would emphatically have been autumn. This year's earliest birds have arrived in the first week of September, and by mid-September, which these days often feels like summer, their flocks can number thousands. Clearly the migratory behaviour of our pinkfeet has changed enormously in these past 150 years.

Today the marsh was quiet and there were no pinkfeet to be seen, so I dawdled through the bracken-scented woodland edge, beset by insects. Field grasshoppers chirruped

September

at the sand track's edge and all along my sunny way were dragonflies: an ominous stack of migrant hawkers around the top of every pine, and common darters locked in tardy mating wheels.

Hoping I might see geese arriving from the sea, I turned north through the dunes. Instead of geese above, I met a sand dune bestiary of plant names at my feet – common cat's-ear, mouse-ear hawkweed, hare's-foot clover, bird's-foot trefoil, common stork's-bill, and the leathery September leaves of hound's-tongue – some in flower for a few weeks more and some now spent.

I reached the fledgling saltmarsh at Holkham Gap, formed since my Norfolk childhood by new dunes hemming in the highest tides, allowing them to drop their finest particles of silt. Here, through winter, dark-bellied brent geese will graze, if left untroubled by dogs off leads and wellied winter hordes of visitors. Brents are our second winter geese to come and they'll be here within a month. Today, though, summer's last brave, brittle flowers of rock sea-lavender marked the marsh's edge.

Back at my bike I heard the pinks again; and, as I pedalled home, so heady was the hedge with ivy that I had to weave and duck to dodge a storm of nectar-drunken wasps.

Monday 14th September

Only a few days after the first of 2020's birds arrived, thousands of geese are roosting on the marsh at Holkham; but just as they did in Stevenson's day, most of them fly out from here to feed. Through the middle of winter, modern pinkfeet are usually found in harvested fields of sugar beet, where they grow fat on what is spilled and spoiled; but the first of the beet will not be lifted for a fortnight yet. So where are these geese feeding now? As with all questions of Holkham geese, I asked Andy Bloomfield.

Son of a Holkham shepherd, Andy was born in the park, where the first geese he loved were the rowdy Egyptians which bred on a pond by his childhood home. Next came feral Canada geese, many of which then nested by the lake. Aged eleven, as his interest in nature grew, he would cycle north through the park to the marshes beyond, running the gauntlet of angry Canada ganders, one of which once knocked him off his bike. In the late 1970s and early 80s, when just 2,000 pinkfeet came to Holkham every year, Andy and his goose-watching confidant, the artist James McCallum from Wells, 'became obsessed quite quickly'. Hardly anyone was interested in geese, except when a rarity was found, but for Andy and James the excitement was never in finding rare geese: 'It was always about the spectacle, the clamour, these birds in a working landscape, the links to the past.' Ever since those days – for many years as a volunteer, and since 2004 as one of Holkham's wardens – Andy has watched and counted the geese and cared for their habitat.

Late this summer, as soon as I began to think of writing on geese, I texted Andy. For he is central to the story of geese at Holkham. He replied immediately, with enthusiasm, inviting me to the marsh. Here in 2006, he said, he and James had counted 90,000 pinkfeet, the largest flock ever to be seen in Norfolk. On the day of my visit in August, Andy drove me out along Bone's Drift to Wroth's Flood, which has become a significant roost for geese in recent years. Though the first of the pinkfeet were still two weeks from arriving, wood sandpipers fidgeted on the mud and fresh young marsh harriers, the colour of melted Bournville, swayed over the marsh. We thought we'd crowned a great day when we found an osprey perching, horizontal like a hammerhead, on a post above the water. But a little further, as I stepped from the truck to close a gate, I startled a juvenile purple heron from a ditch. I yelled to Andy, ahead in the truck, who lifted his camera and framed this lustrous animal in pixels. A juvenile purple heron is melted chocolate too, but Dairy Milk.

Last week I texted Andy again, to ask where Holkham's pinkfeet would be feeding this early in the season. He suggested stubble fields on Beacon Hill, just south of Burnham Market. So this morning I cycled the ten miles to Beacon Hill, in the hope of finding geese. As a teen I cycled hundreds of miles around the Norfolk countryside in search of wildlife; without a helmet, as no one thought to worry in those days. Since then, until this Covid year, I'd lost the simple pleasure of cycling, largely because North Norfolk's roads are now a martyrdom of traffic. But as a cyclist you are so much more alive to landscape than in a car. Your thighs tell you, in a way no driver can ever understand, that Beacon Hill is steep. The bright blooms of common calamint scattered along the bottom of the hedge show you that Norfolk's Late Cretaceous chalk lies close to the surface here. You notice colonies of ivy bees on sandy banks, bustling around your spokes, and hear Roesel's bush-crickets fizzing in the verge.

I saw seven buzzards, circling like a Heathrow planestack above a hillcrest wood, and a kestrel on a telegraph wire, head weighted forward, gaze locked on a hapless rodent in the grass. I saw a young kite low over hedges red and fat with berries, but I found no geese. Instead, I saw a gate where I had stood with friends last winter and had sifted through a mighty flock of pinkfeet. Among them – smaller, darker, orange-legged, round-faced and tiny-billed – a lesser white-fronted goose had fed on harvested beet. On a hot day in September, the memory of this rare and dapper little goose, and of this throng of pinkfeet, made me hunger for the coming winter.

For, as Andy told me last month, in his gentle Norfolk accent, out on Holkham Marsh, 'For me the first pinkfeet are like the first swallows of spring.'

Tuesday 15th September

I was writing today for Norfolk Wildlife Trust, with little time for geese; but halfway through the morning, through the open kitchen door, I heard a greylag's single note. Jumping up, I caught twenty-six of these handsome geese weaving in a lopsided swoosh over my back garden.

I love greylags, in part because they are quite beautiful: corrugated cardboard ruffles down their necks, orange right-angled triangles for bills, and a defiant stare. I love them too because they are ubiquitous. Thank goodness, in this time of widespread loss, for wildlife that is abundant and familiar. In late April, as I walk from my village into town along the river, the ganders stretch their necks at me, tilt up their heads, stick out their jagged tongues and hiss, in defence of bobbly greyish-yellow chicks. Unfashionable as they are, I love them.

Greylags have not always been abundant in Norfolk, nor across the UK. Even in my childhood, being hissed at mere paces from home would have been impossible. For Henry Stevenson, writing in the 1860s, the greylag was a rare winter visitor. He was persuaded though, despite scant evidence, that greylags had been native breeding birds in Norfolk until the wholesale drainage of the East Anglian Fens: 'Taking it then

September

for granted that the grey goose, as well as the bustard, was an indigenous species in Norfolk, the question next arises as to the date when it ceased to inhabit our fens.'

Though a few birds from Iceland and the Scottish islands must always have reached Norfolk in winter, attempts to re-establish the greylag as a breeding species did not begin until the twentieth century. A letter of 1933 from celebrated Norfolk conservationist Dr Sydney Long to the *Eastern Daily Press* appears to document the first release of Hebridean greylags in Norfolk:

'An interesting experiment is now being made by Captain Harry Cator, of Ranworth, to reintroduce the grey lag as a Norfolk breeding species. He has on his broad eight of these birds, full-winged, which were bred in North Uist, in the Outer Hebrides, and so tame have they become that, even with a total stranger, they will eat corn from the hand, allowing their heads to be scratched the while, as I had the pleasure of experiencing a day or so ago.'

He goes on to exhort the wildfowlers of Norfolk not to shoot these friendly geese, should they encounter them. Perhaps they did survive. Certainly, the dashing greylag is now an abundant breeding bird in Broadland, though its presence in Norfolk largely stems from further deliberate introductions. In the 1960s geese were released in North Norfolk by the Wildfowlers' Association of Great Britain and Ireland (now the British Association for Shooting and Conservation), while in the early 70s more were released around Breydon Water, mouth of the Broadland rivers.

As a schoolboy, watching birds across Norfolk in the late 1980s, I never saw a greylag goose. I was thrilled to see my first greylags on a family holiday to Scotland. At Cley, which I visited once or twice a week throughout the year with the country's luckiest school birdwatching club, there were always Canada geese back then, but never greylags.

How things have changed. This morning, as they often do from spring to autumn, greylags have flown calling over my garden. Three weeks ago, when Andy took me onto Holkham Marsh, we drove through a placid herd of greylags, grazing the edge of Wroth's Flood. Some sixty pairs now nest at Holkham, and winter flocks can reach 800 birds. Flashing a grin, Andy told me he resents them because they sound a loud alarm when he approaches Holkham's celebrated heronry. The UK's first colony of spoonbills in almost 400 years has nested here since 2010. Great egrets now breed too; and in 2020 cattle egrets fledged chicks for the first time in Norfolk history. As deep as my love of geese runs, I feel for Andy as his monitoring of these exquisite birds is betrayed each spring by busybody greylags.

Thursday 17th September

The wind swung to the east in the night. As I left home today, just after seven, I questioned my continued insistence on wearing shorts. Only at Cranmer did sweat begin to form between my shoulder blades and where my shades pressed against my face. The wind was no help either, as I cycled on the pockmarked road; and at South Creake Common guinea fowl mocked me from a shabby reclamation yard, their calls like the creaks of my old red bike. I was heading for Beacon Hill again. Andy had been right, of course, and yesterday our mutual friend Ash Saunders saw 900 pinkfeet on the hill. Many were youngsters of the year – in quartets with their parents, just like those I saw at Holkham – giving hope this may have been a good season for them on the Icelandic tundra.

September

At the top of the hill I heard the geese and looked to see them coming from the west like swarms of distant bees. Many hundreds of them came, but banked north to the coast. Searching the crumpled fields below me, I then found many hundreds more; two hundred of them at the far edge of the stubble field by which I stood among the brittle stems of this spring's alexanders. Forty more geese came in from the east, rounding a hilltop wood to approach the birds in the nearest field. Turning to the wind, towards me, they arched their wings and lowered their webbed pink feet, losing height to land with grace on the dun furrows of the harvested crop. At once they blended with the feeding geese. Or seemed to blend, at least, for goose flocks are of fractal complexity. These are not dumb, amorphous hordes. They are families, parents minding young, knowers of geography, surfers of the stars and of the globe's magnetic field. Among the many hundred geese which dappled the fields below me, some had likely been in Iceland just two days back, even now carrying South Icelandic barley in their guts, from stubbles where thousands of their relatives still feed.

The geese, as one, lifted their necks in worry, as a red kite dipped above the fields they fed in. A weakling kite, no threat to healthy geese at all, and yet a hundred of the pinkfeet lifted from the farther field and flew to join those feeding closest to me.

Scanning for more geese in the north, my eyes fell on three fat birds, goldly glowing in the morning sun, on powerlines stretching to Burnham Market: corn buntings, rare now in North Norfolk. I set off to stalk them behind the hedge. Blackberries delayed me first, fat as buntings all along the road, and then two stoats which hurtled from the brambles to the tarmac. I froze and squeaked. One stoat, which in my head I made a boy, came bounding up the road towards me, vanilla-chested, elderberry eyes aglint in the early light.

Then more geese came and more: flocks bunching, recombining, filtering themselves into efficient Vs. I stood, a thin man on a hill amid the thin, spent stems of alexanders, until the last distant skein resolved itself into a quizzical eyebrow in the northern sky.

Thursday 24th September

Winter's first rare goose was reported yesterday: a Todd's Canada goose, seen at great distance with thousands of pinkfeet on the Ribble Estuary in Lancashire. Still known in the UK as Todd's, on their home continent these elegant birds are now more often called interior or Hudson Bay Canada geese, as this is where they nest. Some also breed on Baffin Island, and some as far northeast as western Greenland. The few birds to reach our shores are led here, most likely, by flocks of Greenland-breeding pink-footed geese.

Though plenty of pinkfeet stay in Lancashire the winter long, many among the huge flocks seen crossing Scotland and the northwest in recent days will likely head for Norfolk now. With them will travel the rare geese that they carry. In the absence of your own kind, it is safer, as a lost goose, to flock with birds which at least behave like you. Thus a Todd's Canada goose may well reach Norfolk in the coming days.

I last saw a Todd's at Docking in northwest Norfolk, in December 2016. The huge pinkfoot flock, with which it fed on lifted sugar beet, also held a red-breasted goose. A bird so flawless that it seems enamelled, the redbreast is a rare Siberian visitor, whose world population, almost certainly fewer than 60,000 birds, winters largely in Bulgaria and

September

Romania. A painting by James McCallum of this mighty pinkfoot flock, carrying these two lost geese – from Greenland and Siberia – hangs above my stairs. Shortly after seeing the geese, I spotted James's lovely painting online and knew, though I could ill afford it, that I must own it; so keenly does it capture that bitter day and those wild beings of the Arctic. I wrote to James and went to see the painting a few days later, taking my dearest friend Sarah, who loved it too.

Sarah died the following winter – an expected death, magnificently embraced – and now, whenever I go downstairs, I look on those watercolour geese and think of our great winter pinkfoot flocks, of vagrant geese in Norfolk, of James, and of the blessing of knowing Sarah. Perhaps this winter I shall see a Todd's again – for one is coming – and with me I shall carry Sarah's memory, rare wild goose that she was.

Friday 25th September

A fierce day, it's been today. Since dawn and long before, a northwest wind has hurled itself at Norfolk and unrelenting waves of rain have drenched us. Water has poured for hours down the disused chimney in my kitchen, into a sooty puddle which has marched across my pamment floor. After months of warmth and sun, sparing us the worst privations of the Covid lockdowns, it feels as though the long, gold days of summer at last are done.

I'm bad at winter. I retreat into myself and pine. I came to bed tonight disheartened, brooding on the dark months coming. At twenty to eleven – by some miracle beyond my understanding – I heard, over the raging wind, pinkfeet above my house. I threw a window open to the stormy night and smiled to hear these geese – my geese – arriving, exhausted by the gale.

Wednesday 30th September

A saltmarsh is a paradoxical thing. All coastal landforms result from energy – be it wind, or waves or tide – moving material. Some landforms require huge inputs of energy. A cobblestone beach, as at Sheringham, can only form where waves strike the coast with sufficient rage to push these large flints onto land. A saltmarsh is the opposite. North Norfolk's restless sea carries enormous quantities of silt. These tiny particles are kept afloat by even the weakest waves so – here's the paradox – silt can only settle, to form mudflats and saltmarshes, in the near absence of energy. Such conditions are rare, occurring only at the turn of the tide, in the shelter of a spit or line of dunes, or sometimes at the top of a long, energy-sapping beach.

Where silt is deposited, and not moved on by the following tide, it can be colonised by living things. First algae, adding just a slippery film of stability, then cordgrass and glasswort, which in Norfolk we know (and eat) as samphire. These further fix the silt, adding the rigidity of roots and organic matter harvested as carbon from the atmosphere. Sea aster and saltmarsh grass now colonise, trapping still more silt, raising the marsh just millimetres higher, resisting more effectively the energy of each incoming tide. Next common sea-lavender will grow and, each July, will paint the Norfolk coast with bold Impressionist strokes of mauve.

Where the tide spills over the banks of saltmarsh creeks, the expenditure of energy causes a rampart of silt to be dropped. This is habitat for sea purslane, which likes to grow a few

September

millimetres higher above the salt. It snakes in silvery, distinctive lines across the marsh wherever there's a creek. Finally, inland, as the tired tide runs altogether out of energy, shrubby seablite – beloved of vagrant birds in October gales – grows among sea beet, sea couch grass and perennial sowthistle.

This is an idealised marsh; the kind described in ecology lectures. The real thing, of course, is infinitely complex, product of tides and time, goose-grazing and historic sheep-grazing, bait-digging and storms and seawalls and all the chaos of a billion organisms struggling for life. The real thing is wonderful, one of the defining habitats of coastal Norfolk, and home to the second migrant goose in our web-footed *dramatis personae*: the dark-bellied brent.

For the past few days a raging northwest wind has strafed the Norfolk coast, bringing downpours, fallen trees and little gulls. Throughout it, birders braving the deluge to watch the seabirds windblown to our shore have seen brent geese arriving. Today, the first dry day, I went to where I knew they'd be: Wells Harbour.

My first geese were at Ashburton, the yellow brick Victorian house which all my life has stood alone – a dour Dickensian outpost, a half mile outside Wells – but now stands at the fringe of the growing town. High here, in the wisps of cloud left by the storm, there were pinkfeet. My mind was set on brents though and, even as I chained my bike against the iron railing of the harbour, I heard their reassuring bleat.

Passing a jackdaw flashing me his hard zinc oxide stare, I walked north along the seawall, and found the geese in the channel by the lifeboat house. A few days ago, Andy saw 150 of them here. Today I hastily counted 273. Almost all – but not quite all – were dark-bellied brents, newly here from

Siberia. Just one among the sleepy geese was from elsewhere. Meal white below, in contrast with its coal-black breast and neck, it was a pale-bellied brent goose. I hadn't thought to see one in my first brent flock of the winter, scarce visitors as they are here. Pale-bellies breed widely across the Arctic, with Greenland and east Canadian birds wintering in numbers on the coasts of Ireland and the west of the UK. The few birds reaching Norfolk are thought to come from Svalbard, where I've seen them on the tundra. This population winters typically in Denmark, though also in Northumberland.

I sat on concrete seawall slabs, listening to a grey plover's heartfelt wail, and watching brents. Even as dark-bellies stretched and argued all around it, the waif from Svalbard resolutely slept. I scribbled notes on brents, and on the chimes of redshank and the gently trilling larks, until something spooked the geese, something I never saw. They lifted from the sand, burbling like devout babushkas deep in prayer, and split into two flocks. The smaller group – some seventy birds – flew south towards the town, over Rachael Long's proud Lifeboat Horse. The rest went northwards to the lifeboat house and to the beach, passing in a line above a giant yellow digger and a crowd of workmen in startling orange boiler suits: continent-spanning birds of wind and wild, and our hi-vis attempts to tame it all.

OCTOBER

a thousand pinks

Fierce easterly winds drive both small birds and dark-bellied brent geese to our coast. I speak to a farming relative and to an ornithologist friend about the changing fates of wild geese. By the month's end, with sugar beet harvest underway, great flocks of pinkfeet gather to feed on the spoils, whiffling dramatically as they come to land. Among them there are rarer geese, including stocky tundra beans and dainty barnacles.

Sunday 4th October

Deep in our history someone observed that raindrops would bend light and magnify images. Someone else, no doubt, stoked a fire hot enough to melt sand, making glass. Someone worked out how to mould it. Polish it. Coat it in colourful oxides to capture and focus more light. Thanks to these layers of innovation, and their synergy, I am propelled today by my telescope into the lives of pink-footed geese.

A thousand pinks, at least, are strewn over the field ahead of me, most with their brown heads down among self-seeded cereal shoots growing in bright rills across the stubble. Many of the geese, with mottled mantles, are this year's young, each group attended by two bar-backed birds, their parents.

The Meaning of Geese

There are families of four birds, and families of five. Some sleep, some feed, some stand guard, with a cautious eye on a lone figure and his telescope against a distant hawthorn hedge. For the most part these Icelanders are calm, focused on feeding, oddly quiet for so many garrulous birds together.

The flock's mood changes whenever new groups of geese arrive – fifty, a hundred at a time – their exuberant voices announcing them before I see them in the troubled sky. The field, at New Holkham, which holds the geese, is hemmed in and quite small. To the north are the wall and woods of Holkham Park, while to the south is the high hedge in which I'm hidden. To land here, incoming geese must lose height fast and accurately, and this means whiffling.

If I could learn one thing from geese, it would be to whiffle. To human eyes – this one's at least – whiffling looks such fun. To see a place beneath you where it's safe to land among your kind; and then to drop by twisting side to side, your belly and feet to the sky at the top of each roll. It looks such pure, unbridled fun, yet so controlled. The descending geese switch, in a moment, from wild tumbling to their measured last approach, pink feet stretched wide, webs bright with the little light of this dim day. As they come, they call.

Through my telescope's polished glass, I see these landing geese provoking ripples of reaction in the birds already in the field. Ganders of surrounding families bustle forward stretching necks at newcomers, warning them, I'm sure, to stay away from this year's naïve young. A wider wave of lifted necks moves swiftly through the flock. A male marsh harrier – liver-bodied, silver-winged – is working through the birds, pivoting low above each startled family, needling them for weakness. The harrier is far smaller than the geese; yet time and time again he tries, and many of the pinkfeet

October

jump into flight at his approach. Being tasty, in a world of hawks, is tough.

It was my friends Mark Golley and Lynnette Nicholson who found this pinkfoot flock on Friday, following skeins along farm lanes to track them down. Mark is another of the county's dedicated goose-watchers. Often the sound of his presence at a flock is the soft click of his tally counters – right hand juveniles, left hand adults – as he works from one flank to the other, censusing birds for the Wildfowl and Wetlands Trust. Among the geese on Friday he found a leucistic pinkfoot, pinkish and pale. My interest was sparked, on hearing this, just as Mark's had been in the field. For in the Ribble flock of pinks, which held the Todd's Canada goose last week, three birds of this scarce colour variant were also seen. Could it be that the Ribble flock had already come south to Norfolk, bearing both leucistic pinkfeet and the Todd's? Mark and Lynnette searched thousands of geese on Friday, looking for the Todd's, but mostly for the native joy of watching the first big flock of winter. They did not see the rare Todd's Canada goose, but they kindly told me where to find the flock.

Yesterday a fierce wind from the east brought all-day rain. I couldn't head out on my bike, no matter that birds were raining too: song thrushes, chiffchaffs, blackcaps, robins, goldcrests, all along the coast. With the promise of fine weather, last night I set my alarm for six. When I woke today, the weather was good, but overnight the forecast had morphed to persistent rain. I silenced my alarm and turned in bed, while Radio Four agreed that heading out today I would be soaked.

I snoozed but couldn't help remembering a line from *Wintering*, Stephen Rutt's lovely account of his own season spent with geese. 'We have learned that we cannot wait for good weather to do things. We have learned that to do and see anything here involves a good coat and a belligerence towards bad weather.'

I made myself get up, pull on long trousers and boots for the first time this autumn. For the first time also, I clipped panniers to the frame which was fixed last week on the back of my bike, and stuffed them with my scope, tripod, binoculars, coat and more. For the first time I was fully ready for a winter of geese on my bike.

Then, quite as nobly as a migrant goose, I fancied, I launched into October's mild and generous rain, cycling up the Dry Road – not dry at all today – until the turning for New Holkham. Puffing up pink cottages hill at Egmere, where Ash once saw a wintering snow goose from the Wells school bus, I looked up to see a squadron of golden plovers just above the road. Mostly though I lowered my head, tipped water off my helmet to my thighs, and forced my wet way forward to the geese.

So here I am, in the corner of a rain-soaked field, rooks gargling overhead. Behind me in the hedge, above my sodden bicycle, there is a busy flock of greenfinches. Among them I can hear the hard snarl of a brambling, newly here. In front of me the field moves gently with a crop of geese, found here on Friday by Lynnette and Mark. My phone chimes in my pocket. My cousin must have driven by me on the road. 'Not the nicest weather for cycling!' she says. But, here among the geese, it is.

Wednesday 7th October

On this very date in 1758, in the rectory of the North Norfolk village of Burnham Thorpe, Catherine Suckling

October

was making anxious preparations. She had given birth on 29th September to her sixth child, a boy. The newborn was weak and sickly and it was feared he might not live for long. Thus he was to be baptised on 8th October, by the rector, Catherine's husband, and given the name Horatio.

Many of the cottages and farmhouses, built of jumbled chalk and Norfolk brick, past which I cycled in Burnham Thorpe this morning would have been known to the future Lord Nelson during his childhood here. Perhaps some of the rugged hawthorns in the tall hedge north of the village were also here in his day. Nelson would even have recognised the vernacular style, in the same chalk and gentle orange brick, of the new houses being built in the village today; and the donkeys grazing the meadow in the little valley of the Burn would have been familiar.

Young Horatio must also have known the marshes of Burnham Overy and Holkham, where my bike and I were bound this morning, as they lie just two miles north of his childhood home. As a country boy, it's likely he knew their wildlife too. I would like to think that in Nelson's day the marshes were grazed by handsome Norfolk horn sheep. Beside them, in autumn and in winter, pink-footed geese must surely have grazed, between flights to feed in cereal stubbles and on spoiled potatoes in nearby fields. Perhaps on the day of Nelson's christening, just as today, there were lines of pinkfeet above his now-demolished home. The villagers would not have called them pinkfeet though, for the pink-footed goose would not be described as a species (separate from the bean goose) until the 1830s.

I had cycled to Burnham Thorpe through New Holkham, in the hope of seeing Sunday's pinkfoot flock again, but the birds had gone. I stopped by the lone cottage at the empty

The Meaning of Geese

field's edge, as much to ask the woman in the drive about geese as about the number on her gate. How was it that her house, orphaned by a field, with no other building in sight save the park's south wall, could be number 74? She chuckled, explaining that it was a keeper's cottage and that the number carried over from the nearest houses in the park. And the geese that had so recently been her neighbours? 'They seem to have gone now,' she replied.

So I went too, this time up the west flank of the park, saluting Nelson as I rode through Burnham Thorpe. At the edge of the village I heard the happy talk of pinkfeet and stopped to scan this wild week's one blue sky. I found them, high above me, heading west, and counted thirty-two, loud in the clichéd puffs of cloud. I stood and gazed, amazed to see this thing I've known my whole life long, these geese from Iceland, shouting in my Norfolk sky.

Nelson's sky too. A half mile from his birthplace, these were the many-times grandchildren of geese he must have heard and seen, eaten perhaps, in the fields and marshes of our blessed stretch of coast. Every year since young Horatio walked these chalky lanes, pinkfeet have travelled north to Iceland, nested on the frosty upland tundra, and brought their young to winter in our muddy Norfolk.

Reaching the coast road, I leaned my bike against the brambles frothing through an abandoned gate. I trained my scope on Burnham Overy Dunes and on the distant freshmarsh of the Holkham National Nature Reserve, where hundreds of pinkfeet were gathered. Slowly, as I stood and chatted to a friend who happened by, the geese began to peel away, bound inland to feed. Low above our heads they went, towards the stubbles of Beacon Hill, group after group; honeyed breasts shining in the welcome autumn sun, excited voices dropping to our ears and to the wet October earth.

I had cycled along roads worn, paved and tarmacked by human convention stretching back centuries before Nelson was born. But the geese, how do they know which way to head, which fields to visit? I'd passed many stubbled acres in the morning, all of which looked right for geese to me. All were empty. Which among the geese decides a field is good to feed in, safe to land in? How do geese in these coastal marshes know where their relatives are feeding, five, eight, ten miles inland? There will be much to wonder in the coming winter, as I speak to scientists, to Norfolk's dedicated goose-watchers, to friends whose geolocator tags spy on pinkfeet as they fly from Iceland's endless summer days to Norfolk's few dull hours of winter light. Many of these things no one yet understands. Mysteries, to a lover of the wild, are good.

I stumbled across one more mystery as I pedalled home. At the New Holkham junction with the Dry Road, I cycled straight across, onto Crabbe Road, and east to Wighton, looking for sugar beet fields which will soon be harvested and might therefore soon hold geese. In doing so I crossed from the valley of the Burn to the valley of the Stiffkey, the little river near whose source stands the old flint farmhouse in which I was raised. Halfway along the road I started to see cars pulled onto verges. Puzzled, I remembered that, as they were driving home from revisiting their New Holkham flock of geese on Sunday, Mark and Lynnette had seen a hoopoe here. I had assumed it gone; but, huddled behind a hawthorn hedge, marvelling at this crazy-crested bird just feet in front of them, a dozen birders and photographers crouched and stood.

How, I wondered, could this outlandish bird, which breeds nowhere in Britain and winters nowhere in northern Europe, come to be on a Wighton muckheap in October. How could it have so misjudged migration? Pondering the feathered throng hurtling through our skies at this wild and wind-wracked time of year, I pushed my pedal down, south along the River Stiffkey through Little Walsingham and Great Snoring, and on to the River Wensum, by which I live.

Wednesday 14th October

I used to imagine, as a child, that each of us trailed a silken thread wherever we went. Our threads would change in colour with our moods, telling the story both of our comings and goings and of our feelings. Together we wove a huge – and endless – tapestry of our interconnected lives.

This forgotten fantasy came to me today, as Gav and I spent hours with migrant birds pouring to the Norfolk coast from the North Sea's metalled sky. Gav Horsley's silk thread and mine have intertwined for more than thirty years. He is the eldest son of the biology teacher who would drive a wide-eyed pack of boys downhill from Holt to Cley each week to teach us about wildlife. Gav and I have seen countless Norfolk birds together, over many years, and he still comes home for more whenever he finds the time.

Last night the wind shifted to the east, and will stay in that quarter for several days to come: perfect conditions for birds to drop to our coast on their migration. Gav and I resolved to meet early this morning at Stiffkey, and to spend the day in search of migrant birds. He is a singer in London, and 2020 – the opera houses closed – has not been kind. His thread had brightened, I imagined, as he travelled home last night, in readiness for autumn easterlies and the birds that they might bring.

My own thread too has been dull in recent days. I'm tired. For the past week I have worked hard on urgent articles and a film. As I cycled the thirteen miles north to the coast today, weaving across the chalky valley of the River Stiffkey, my legs worked hard but my thread grew brighter at the thought of a day in the easy company of my childhood friend.

North of Copys Green, where Mrs Temple's brown Swiss cows peered at my happy red bicycle through the fences of their fields, my legs had a break. Cycling between the great hedges of the lane I could hear pinkfeet clamouring nearby. Small groups squiggled low above me; but not nearly enough to be making such a noise. When I reached a break in the hedge at last, I crept round the corner and saw thousands of bustling geese. They saw me too, despite my care, as the nearest birds were right by the gap. A yapping pulse ripped through the flock as they took to the air. Most times I would feel mortified to have startled them; but the crop was winter wheat, where geese are considered a threat to the farmer's yield, so they would soon have been scared away, deliberately, by someone else. For the first time in this winter of geese, I stood in awe at the volume of birds in the sky beyond the field: volume in numbers and volume in sound.

At Stiffkey, for want of anywhere else, I chained my bike to the National Trust sign and launched into the wind-sculpted wood, to find both birds and my lifelong friend. First though, among blackbirds, redwings and chaffinches, I met the artist James McCallum, his eyes bright with the promise of the day ahead. We spoke about geese, of course, of brents arriving and the pinks I had seen as I cycled north. We spoke about cycling and Norfolk's gruelling hills. And we talked of the woodcock and fieldfares he'd seen just minutes before with Gav.

I found Gav on the far flank of the wood, haloed in goldcrests, which were low among blooming ivy and tar-spotted sycamore leaves. These nothing-sized birds had not been here when he'd passed a moment before. They had just arrived from the sea and the sky and the resinous needles of Scandinavia. Their fear overcome by hunger, they fed beside us, and squeaked. They were the first of thousands of birds we saw together today; each tailed, in my mind, by the coloured thread of its journey southwest from the taiga.

We walked by lanes where dozens of blackbirds fed and by fields where hundreds of handsome redwings hopped, my first warm-chested fieldfares with them too. We saw chaffinch flocks, in Holkham's quinoa and *Phacelia* strips; and among them greenfinches, bramblings, linnets and stammering yellowhammers. Brambles and hawthorns, the length of our walk, were busy with robins and dunnocks and wrens. And goldcrests, everywhere goldcrests.

This was a day of friendship and of wonder: of thousands of migrant lives brought here by wind, genes, instinct and the planet's axial tilt. And in my child self's mind, these many birds, from all across the north, together wove a vast and humbling tapestry along our glorious Norfolk coast.

Friday 16th October

As Gav and I walked on Wednesday, we mostly searched the sheltered southern side of hedges and stands of trees, for this is where exhausted migrants gather. To our north,

October

the whole day, there was saltmarsh, peopled by redshank, curlew and golden plover, all stirred, time and again, by a young male peregrine. Sometimes he came low from fields inland, sometimes he tore through the distant dunes of Stiffkey Binks, but always he was close. Unperturbed, small flocks of dark-bellied brent geese grazed the saltmarsh all along our way.

It was to these brents that my thoughts returned today. Last night a photo appeared on Twitter of a black brant, taken among dark-bellied brents in the harbour channel at Wells. Most handsome among brent geese, black brants are from the North Pacific. All the familiar features of a dark-bellied brent goose seem somehow heightened on these striking birds. Whereas dark-bellies are a cold lead grey on their backs and undersides, black brants are bitter chocolate black, with the warm cast of a second-day bruise. Thanks to this, their solid black breasts and necks contrast less strongly with their bodies than in dark-bellied brents. The white parts of a black brant are exaggerated too. Their collars are broader and meet in a lacy white triangle under their chins. Their flank patches, sometimes hardly there on a dark-bellied brent, are broad and boldly white.

This is the theory of black brants but, just like the saltmarsh they frequent, in the real world they are greatly more complex. Black brants do arrive here – lost from the Pacific tundra – and in Norfolk invariably they are with our coastal flocks of dark-bellied brents. Here some of them fall in love. As geese form lifelong pair bonds, it is perhaps not too poetic to call their courtship love. Come spring, the genetic and magnetic forces that try to pull the brant back to the Pacific are overcome by this pair bond, formed on our Norfolk mud. The brant ends up in western Siberia with its dark-bellied mate and together, in Taymyr perhaps, they may raise chicks. In autumn, around the middle of October, they come back with their young to Norfolk. Here the fun begins. First-generation hybrids between black brants and dark-bellied brents can be astonishingly similar to brants, lacking only the rich chocolate tones of the mantle and belly. These birds, and presumably their own offspring, plus the fickle light of a Norfolk winter, lend endless complexity to the task of identifying a true black brant.

Last night, when the Wells brant's photo appeared online, my goose-watching friends were split over its identity. Some thought it was a hybrid, but wanted to see it in life to be sure. Others were persuaded it was the real thing. This morning I got on my bike and cycled to Wells to see for myself.

I did not see. I checked hundreds of dark-bellied brents but could find no brant or anything like a brant. What I did see was better by far. At the pipe which drains from the freshmarsh into the harbour channel, I saw my first juvenile dark-bellied brents of this autumn. Seeing them, I smiled. Juvenile brents have a sock-puppet look and neat white bars on their backs. They and their parents are just arriving, three weeks after the first of the brents which failed to breed this year. These families bring a bickering energy to the flocks; fathers stretching their stout black necks and running across the sand at geese which wander too close to their young. There were several families with three youngsters in the harbour today, some with four, and one, that I could see, with five. The two biggest families that James McCallum has ever seen, he tells me, had brought eight young with them from the tundra.

I spent two hours today, just being with brents, watching the ganders' bravado, and the gentler way the mothers

October

shadowed their young. I listened as burbling groups of geese came and went from the sand, as grey plovers wailed in the marsh and a busy turnstone rattled by. A redshank nimbly picked along the shore, round mooring chains draped with algae by the ebbing tide; and the saltmarsh, stretching all the way to Blakeney church, where my parents were wed, was dappled red with the autumn colour of samphire, and spotted black with the necks of hundreds of brents.

Out there somewhere was a brant, or something like one. Perhaps our paths will cross in the coming months. For today, just being with dark-bellied brents was enough.

Thursday 22nd October

My great-grandmother Muriel Case was one of a dozen children, the youngest of whom was Brian. His grandson David Lyles farms at Muckleton, a little to the south of Burnham Market; in goose country. For the past four days I have been working in King's Lynn. On my way home today I stopped to visit my distant relative and to hear of his life with geese.

David and his late father took the farm as tenants in 1957, but purchased it some thirty years ago. Over six decades at Muckleton, David has witnessed radical changes in food production, and their disastrous impacts on the landscape. From his North Norfolk glacial moraine he has reflected, and acted, on the state of his land and the plight of the wildlife with which he shares it.

David is a far from ordinary Norfolk farmer now, but he began his career with another mindset. His was a farming generation bent on mechanisation and productivity. As a young man, along with almost every other farmer, he laced the land with DDT, and with a string of chemicals sold to him as perfectly safe; just, he notes, as neonicotinoids are sold as safe in much of the world today.

The start of his conversion to wildlife-friendly farming came when he planted a strip of woodland in a cereal crop yet to be harvested. In a line of traps among the saplings he killed a number of weasels. Later that year, when he lost ten acres of sugar beet on the stony hill above the wood to mice, he reasoned that the weasels, had he only left them, would have helped suppress the mice.

The farm is a different place today, where space is made for wildlife. Not left, but made. During the two hours we walked across his land, David explained his many innovations for wildlife and the frustration he feels when government agencies and NGOs don't, to his mind, go far enough. Year round his lovely farm is home to foxes, badgers, polecats, tree sparrows and corn buntings. Stone curlews and turtle doves nest in summer and most years in the past ten Montagu's harriers have bred here too. 'Two years ago they nested right here,' he told me, pointing at the flinty ground beneath a strip sown with plants for birds and bees.

We sat in a breezy tower hide and talked of geese, though only once a barn owl had left its roost in the rafters. From here we overlooked the chalky ridge of David's farm, and the fields to which ecologists from the University of Hull lure pink-footed geese with decoys, to be caught under licence in cannon nets. Some of the geese are ringed with British Trust for Ornithology metal rings alone, some fitted with lettered neck collars for identification in the field, and some with geolocators, allowing their movements to be charted via the mobile network. Thus David has a privileged view into the lives of the geese which visit his

October

farm. He admits to sentimentality when he sees old friends returning to his land, bringing their young of the year from the uplands of Iceland.

David's love and knowledge of geese stretch back as long as he has lived here. In the 1960s he saw pinkfeet return to their traditional North Norfolk haunts. They had fled to the Wash – he believes – following World War Two when disturbed by artillery along our coast. Since then he has counted more and more geese on the farm, and on surrounding land, with numbers building steeply from the 1970s. In the 1960s beet was still lifted one row at a time, by a harvester, pulled by a horse or tractor, which popped each swollen root from the ground as it went. The beet was topped by hand with a hook, leaving little for geese to glean. Over subsequent decades, beet has been harvested by ever larger machines, lifting two rows at a time, three rows, six, nine, and today as many as twelve. These mechanised harvesters slice the top off the beet in the field, where it's left. Pinkfeet have fed on these nutritious, sugary tops throughout my goose-watching life, and over this time their numbers in Norfolk have risen enormously, in line with their global population; until just a few years ago when beet farming began to change again.

When pinkfeet arrive in September, the beet is still in the ground. As I saw on Beacon Hill last month, they feed on self-seeded cereals, or on grass in coastal marshes. Once beet begins to be lifted, in late September or, as this year, thanks to drought, in early October, Norfolk pinkfeet shift to feeding on tops. However, as David explained today, economic pressure to drill wheat early means farmers now plough beet fields almost as they are harvested, leaving our geese with nothing to eat. Geolocators, and the evidence of our own eyes, reveal that, starved of North Norfolk beet, many geese now undertake what David terms a mini-migration to the fields and marshes of the Norfolk Broads. When I was a young birder, there were no pinkfeet in the Broads. Now they are abundant. Likewise, these days many pinks, Andy Bloomfield and James McCallum have told me, stay in Lancashire or Scotland all winter long; so our Norfolk flocks have declined significantly from a peak a decade or so ago. The cause, they believe, is this change in the beet harvest; though I suspect the sinister hand of climate change – known to have shortened the migrations of many waterfowl – must also be involved.

Beet was being lifted on David's neighbour's farm, twelve rows at a time, as we sat and talked in his hide today. His own beet was still in the ground, in what has been known as Goose Field since long before his tenure here. When it comes to be lifted, David will sit in the hide, as he has over many years past, and watch pinkfoot scouts fly inland to find safe fields in which to feed. If they like what they see, the scouts will land. If startled, they'll fly on, giving a warning call. I asked about communication between the geese, posing the question I had asked myself a few days ago while watching pinkfeet leaving Burnham Overy Dunes. 'I have a drone,' David replied. 'From 200 feet up I can see all the way to Old Hunstanton. The geese see each other for miles around.'

David's love and understanding of the wildlife on his farm run deep, and for years he has encouraged his neighbours to make space for wildlife on their land too. 'I used to feel people thought I was crazy,' he said, showing me a dense hedge planted for nesting birds, with *Buddleja* for butterflies and bees. 'Now I feel people are more on my side.'

October

Saturday 24th October

Six years before David Lyles and his father Roger took on their North Norfolk farm, the modern study of pink-footed geese began. In 1951 Peter Scott made a groundbreaking expedition to central Iceland, accompanied by his future wife Philippa Talbot-Ponsonby, by renowned ornithologist James Fisher, and the eminent Icelandic ecologist Finnur Gudmundsson. The story of their expedition is told by Scott and Fisher in *A Thousand Geese*, which I finished reading last night.

At the time it was only quite recently that nesting pinkfeet had been documented by science: in Spitsbergen in 1855, in Greenland in 1891 and in Iceland in 1929. By the end of World War Two, the Spitsbergen and Greenland populations had been preliminarily censused, leaving ornithologists wondering where the bulk of the British winter birds bred. Scott and Fisher believed the answer might lie in Iceland.

In October 1950, under the auspices of his newly formed Severn Wildfowl Trust (now the Wildfowl and Wetlands Trust), Peter Scott had pioneered cannon-netting to capture and mark pink-footed geese in Scotland, in the hope of seeing the same birds in Iceland a few months later. *A Thousand Geese* recounts the summer of 1951, which Scott and his colleagues spent in the tundra along the Þjórsá River, observing and ringing pink-footed geese.

To reach the Þjórsá, the explorers rode for several days on Icelandic ponies, unsure, so early in the summer – with rivers in spate and the tundra not yet green enough to feed the ponies – that they would even make their intended camp. They succeeded, and their long stay among gyrfalcons, purple sandpipers, whooper swans and thousands of pink-footed geese was an untrammelled success. They watched snow buntings fledge from a crack in an ancient wall, recorded the flowers of the tundra as the summer sun teased them into bloom, and they ringed 1,151 geese, far more than they had dared to hope was possible.

That same autumn Scott returned to Scotland, to see whether their efforts in Iceland would shed light on the lives of UK-wintering geese. His team caught 530 pinkfeet, nine of them with rings from their expedition to the Þjórsárver. The foundations had been laid for decades of study of Icelandic geese by the Wildfowl and Wetlands Trust.

Sunday 25th October

There are days in Norfolk's autumn when the ten-day gloom breaks and egg-yolk light oozes across the landscape, basting everything it touches. Today was such a day. Last night, seeing the forecast, I set my alarm for dawn. This week hundreds of pinkfeet have been seen by the end of Lady Anne's Drive at Holkham; and yesterday Andy texted to say that 12,000 had been censused at roosts along the Norfolk coast, and with them the first wild barnacle geese of winter. It was time my bike and I went back to Holkham to see for ourselves.

There were no geese along Lady Anne's Drive as I arrived, save a few greylags and here and there a pair of thug-eyed Egyptians; but as I drew to a halt – railing against geese and their inconstancy – I saw them: thousands of specks, filling the sky above Wells and heading my way. This was the largest flock by far that I have seen since the geese arrived last month. I leaned my bike against

October

a cross-hatched poplar trunk and looked up as the geese thronged from the east, wave after shouting wave. I willed them to land in the marshes along the drive, where I could see them, watch them, learn.

They did not. Some flew over, noisily, dropping to fields south of the pines, towards Burnham Overy Dunes. Most landed beyond the seawall northeast of Lady Anne's Drive, at the back of a field and into the rising sun. Watching geese, I quickly realised, would not be easy today. I did my best. I took my scope and tripod from the panniers on my bike and scanned every group that I could see, but the light was cruel and the birds too far. Had there been a barnacle goose among them — daintier and black-and-white — I would have seen it, but I had no chance of finding a tundra bean goose, several of which have been seen along the Norfolk coast in recent days. Tundra beans are far too similar to pinkfeet to pick out at distance, against early morning light. I gave up on the geese, content to have seen and heard my first huge flock of autumn. Just as I did, the phone in my pocket buzzed. It was my dear friend Joe.

Joe Beckham is the best birder I know. He has not seen the longest list of birds; far from it. He is not the most skilled at finding rare birds, or even identifying common ones by sight or sound. He does not spend longest in the field. But he loves birds best. Joe is a puppy — all enthusiasm, energy and warmth — and when he talks of birds he beams. At the start of the first Covid lockdown he made a WhatsApp group among our local birding friends. For two months, as spring birds poured into Norfolk, we shared news of what we were seeing at home, and shared jokes on the strange new world in which we suddenly lived. It was important to us all.

'Where are you?' he asked. 'I'm in the village car park.' So I cycled south from the marsh to the grandiose gates of Holkham Park and met him. Two days ago, Andy found a drake ring-necked duck on Holkham Lake, among hundreds of tufted ducks. A ring-necked duck is our tufted duck's North American doppelgänger and just a few are seen in the British Isles each year, mostly in the west. Joe had never seen one, so together we walked through October-golden woods to the lake. I love ducks quite as much as I love geese, and Joe loves everything, so it was joy on this shining day to sift with him through tufted ducks, pochard, mallard and pencil-chested gadwall, looking for one lost bird.

We found him, admired him at length, comparing his jaunty, cocked-up tail with the shorter tails of the tufted ducks, and his shallower, ski-jump forehead and longer bill. He was busy, far busier than the many tufted ducks around him, preening and bathing and bustling the length of the flock. To find a rarity among geese, experienced watchers say, you should check the edges of flocks for birds on the move, as though searching for someone like them.

Perhaps our ring-necked duck – so similar in appearance to the tufted ducks, but an ocean apart in origin – was looking for someone like him.

Monday 26th October

The work begun by Peter Scott and friends in Iceland in 1951 continues to this day. Among today's key players is my friend Kane Brides, research officer at the Wildfowl and Wetlands Trust. Until 2020 Kane had visited Iceland every year for fifteen years – once for a ten-month stretch – in pursuit of geese and whooper swans, and an understanding of their lives.

Kane and I spoke last month by Zoom, as my autumn with geese began, and we talked again today. In the meantime I have pestered him by text with many questions. He greets my queries with his broad, handsome smile and a similarly broad knowledge of Iceland's geese. Since lockdown began in spring he has been at home with family in Manchester, away from his Slimbridge desk and away from his pinkfeet in the mountains of central Iceland and the greylags which breed more widely across the island.

Though some non-breeding birds may stay for two months more, pinkfeet bound for Iceland typically leave Norfolk by the end of February. In recent years many have left even earlier. Most of these northbound geese, Kane tells me, will stop in Lancashire, sometimes for several weeks, but by the end of March they leave the UK, flying northwest over the Hebrides to Iceland, which they reach from the first week of April. Our pinkfeet must now wait in Iceland while the tundra of the central mountains thaws. Their eggs will be laid in May and incubation may not begin until the end of the month. Often these waiting geese gather in fields in the south of Iceland, just as they did before flying south in autumn.

WWT and its partners estimate that the Iceland and Greenland population of pink-footed geese stands at over 500,000 birds, almost all of which winter in the UK. This represents a more than tenfold increase in population from the 30 or 40,000 birds considered to be wintering in the UK by Peter Scott and James Fisher in 1951. UK agriculture, Kane says, is thought to be the main cause of this explosion. Fattened in our fields over winter, more and more birds return in peak condition to Iceland, where their breeding sites are better protected too. It is little wonder that the impacts of pinkfeet on Icelandic farmers have risen steeply over these past seventy years.

A female pink-footed goose lays a clutch of three to five eggs which she incubates for twenty-six or twenty-seven days, while her male stands guard nearby. Once hatched, the two parents shepherd their chicks to nearby wetlands, where they feed on aquatic vegetation and on crowberries which – Kane chuckles as he tells me – stain the goslings' droppings pink. Many nests, he says, are lost to great and Arctic skuas, and many chicks to Arctic foxes. Gyrfalcons probably take them too, he muses, though snowy owls, such as the one seen close to camp by Scott and Fisher in 1951, are very rare as Icelandic breeding birds.

In late June or July each year, Kane joins a team of Icelandic ornithologists for the annual round up of moulting geese. Exceptionally among birds, waterfowl – which can retreat to water for safety – moult all their flight feathers at once, rendering them flightless. In 1951 the expedition's members chased the geese on horseback or charged headlong on foot into icy water after them. Today, late summer's flightless flocks, largely of non-breeding or failed breeding birds, are deftly herded by Kane and his colleagues into a corral on the tundra. Whereas Peter Scott's ringing campaign in 1951 took weeks to accomplish, the team can now catch and ring three or four hundred birds in a day, taking advantage of summer's round-the-clock daylight.

As with David's cannon-netted geese at Muckleton, all Icelandic birds are given a metal ring on one leg. Some are given Darvic neck-collars, with unique codes which can be read by birders and scientists in the field. Some are given

October

Darvic leg-rings, also with unique codes. Just a few are fitted with geolocators.

Kane and his WWT colleagues currently follow fifty tagged pink-footed geese via the mobile network, even sending operational instructions to their geolocators by text. All of these tagged pinks are female. Waterfowl, exceptionally among birds, can reliably be sexed in the hand from their vents. A tagged female goose provides greatly better information than a male. As only females incubate, a tagged bird which sits still for twenty-six days in May and June is hugely likely to be on eggs. If she then stays within a small area for several weeks, it is probable that she has hatched chicks and that at least some of them have survived. This works well for birds in Iceland, where the mobile network is excellent, but in Greenland, where some geese from the same population also breed, the network is poor. Pinkfeet nest only in the southeast of Greenland but, counterintuitively, many birds which fail to breed in Iceland – their eggs lost to skuas or their chicks snatched by foxes – hop to northeast Greenland for their post-breeding moult. Here their geolocators can vanish from the mobile network for weeks on end, until they next pass an Icelandic or even Scottish mobile mast and their data are downloaded for WWT to see.

Greenland breeders, Icelandic breeders which moult in Greenland, and birds which spend the whole summer in Iceland all join the same winter flocks in the UK (whereas the 78,000 birds from the separate Svalbard population winter largely in Belgium, Germany and Denmark). The northeast of Greenland, where many pinkfeet moult, is home to muskoxen, walruses and polar bears. Since geolocator-tagged geese which winter in Norfolk have been known to visit Greenland, and since the birds' southward migration is often swift, I would like to believe that, among the flocks I saw reaching Norfolk in September, there were birds which had stood just days before in the mighty pawprints of polar bears.

In my mind it is possible at least. I have no plans to ask whether Kane's geolocators prove me wrong.

Wednesday 28th October

My old friend Martin Hayward Smith appeared yesterday at the blue front door of my little flint house. 'Hello old bean,' he said, as he always does. 'Would you like to go to the houseboat tomorrow? I'll pick you up at 9:30.'

So today at 9:30 I climbed into his venerable green Land Rover ('the only vehicle I've ever had that's gone up in value') and together we drove north along little lanes, past the looming bulk of Binham Priory, and up a muddy track, squeezed between dense stands of European gorse and a zany hedge of the Duke of Argyll's teaplant. At the end of it, on a tiny patch of grass among half-forgotten boats, Martin parked.

'Follow the anchor chain,' he said, as we waded into Freshes Creek, the mouth of the River Stiffkey, by which I grew up eight miles to the south. Two rock pipits landed at the creek's edge as we squelched, their feathers of one dull colour with the miles of mud around us. 'I've had houseboats here for twenty-five years,' Martin said, unlocking the wooden hatch on The Marsh Boat. 'She's my third, and last.' He placed a rough ladder against the side of the boat for me to climb. 'The only rule,' he said, 'is no wellies inside or on the roof. If you need to wee, just go in the creek down there. The tide flushes it twice a day.'

October

Out in the marsh a bait-digger worked, his spaniel by his side, but otherwise no human was in sight; just the wide, wild marsh stretching from Wells to Blakeney, and beyond to Sheringham Park. To the northeast, the long arm and crooked hand of Blakeney Point embraced our whole horizon. 'Let's go for a walk,' said Martin, and we set off north, over sand and mud towards the sea.

A coastline is all change, always, but of two kinds. There is cyclical change: twice a day the moon's gravity, and sometimes the sun's, drag the sea towards land and over its edges. Likewise, at the same time each year, the waning days bring wilder weather to the coast, and rougher storms. There is linear change too. Waves largely strike this northern stretch of the Norfolk coast from the northeast, but gravity drags them back to the sea by the shortest route, straight down the beach. In this way – the longshore drift of GCSE geography – sand, rocks and gravel carried by the waves are moved westwards along our coast. Thus Scolt Head Island and Blakeney Point are stretched each year a little further to the west. Martin's marsh, sheltered behind the Point, has altered greatly in the many years that he has known it. Lately more sand has been brought here by the sea, he told me as we crossed a new ridge, woven in place by sand couch grass, with sea sandwort stitched along its seaward edge. Further out, in the mud at the fringe of the harbour, there were many small islands of cordgrass. 'They were never here until recently,' Martin said.

The shelduck, scattered like beads from a broken necklace across the mud, have always been here in winter, though, and the many brent geese among them too. Four red-breasted mergansers were in the channel joining the North Sea and Blakeney Pit, and grey seal bulls, wet noses shining in the

The Meaning of Geese

morning sun. More seals were at the channel's edge, on the Morston side: greys and some kind-faced harbour seals, their tails curled up from the sand. We walked on past them to the sea, because the sea demanded it. 'I come because out here everything fades away,' said Martin.

I had come to be in the habitat of geese. I have seen thousands of geese this autumn, but always from the edges of their lives, and looking in. Today, thanks to Martin's long anchor-hold in this untamed place, I was in the geese's world. All across the sand and mud were brent goose droppings: long, cylindrical, spinach-green and tipped in white. Around them, everywhere, the small, neat web-prints of these dark Siberian visitors. The geese themselves were grazing in the pit, on eelgrass exposed by the same low tide which had let us come here, into their lives. A sanderling dropped to the wet sand beside us, giving its chiming call. Another landed with it, and for a moment sang; its lark-like twitter – above the mounting southwest wind – taking me to summer tundra. To our north, apart from turbines, which Martin has also witnessed sprouting here, nothing stood between that tundra and the two of us, and our lonely, brine-filled bootprints on a Norfolk beach.

The brents were not the only geese we saw today. The moon will be full on Saturday, so pinkfeet now feel safe to feed inland by night, and come to roost on the shore by day. On the distant sand towards Wells there were thousands of pinks, though a lone man at the fringe of the East Hills kept them edgy. Later, as we feasted on Martin's picnic in his houseboat, drinking steaming mugs of tea, the pinks flew off above us, heading to the fields, dropping sharp calls to the tidal mud and sand, to the battered sea purslane and the fleshy leaves of sea-lavender all around us. I looked to Martin as he washed the dishes, outside in this bright day's only wave of drizzle. 'You're good at life,' I said. My old friend smiled, with one last sea aster flowering close to his welly's toe.

Friday 30th October

'Huge flock of pinkfeet,' a text from Ash Saunders announced last night. 'In harvested maize southeast of Wells. More than ten thousand birds, all roosting on the Binks.'

I shelved plans for today. With such a flock in easy cycling distance – and the next day forecast to be dry – everything else would have to wait. This morning at eight I took to the roads on my bike, weaving round rainwater puddles as I pedalled north. At the Golden Gates, on the eastern edge of Holkham Park, I turned east through a belt of woodland, along an unmade track, my bike and bones juddering over thousands of protruding flints. Beyond the woods I started to hear geese, and then to see them, dark lines across the morning's scarcely less dark sky.

The first geese were in a winter cereal field north of the track, thousands of them, resting. I stopped to scan, dumping my bike in the long grass; but groups of them were lifting from the field, wheeling over the hedge, to the maize that Ash had mentioned in the next field to the east. I cycled on, to the entrance of this muddy maize field, the back of which held an Arctic harvest: thousands of pink-footed geese.

For almost six hours I stood by the hedge, peering through my scope, into the lives of geese. For almost six hours I was that skinny boy again, consumed by these handsome birds and their behaviour; these lifelong friends whose high Icelandic chatter has been the sound of all my Norfolk winters.

The Meaning of Geese

The bulk of the geese, of course, were pinkfeet. As Stephen Rutt writes in *Wintering*, 'They are the base goose, the one from which the others deviate.' Pinkfeet are medium-sized, which means nothing if geese are not part of your daily lives. They are larger than brent geese and barnacles but smaller than greylags and Canadas. Nicely medium-sized. They are medium-coloured too, not so dark as dark-bellied brent geese, nor so pale as greylags, nor so patterned as barnacles, Canadas or pale-bellied brents. The base goose, as Stephen says, yet lovely, and endlessly varied.

A pinkfoot's shoulder feathers are a gentle bluish grey, finely tipped with buff. This blue is clearest when the goose is on the wing, when the colour can be seen to bleed into the darker flight feathers. The goose's head and neck are a warm dark brown – cocoa-dusted – and, just as the silky grey of its back blends with the brown of its neck, so too the brown neck fades into the goose's paler breast and belly, which are warm buff, darker and blotchier on the flanks. The only bold contrasts on a pinkfoot's plumage are with its pure white vent and its white tail marked with a blue-grey bar of the same colour as its rump. The bill is dark brown, a shade darker than the face, with a prominent bright pink spot on the upper mandible. Sometimes this is a neat blob, close to the tip of the bill, folding just far enough down the sides to touch the lower mandible. Sometimes this pink stretches back along the bill towards the nostrils. Sometimes, especially on young birds, it is barely there; and often, on birds feeding in muddy beet fields, it can barely be seen.

A pinkfoot's legs and feet, unsurprisingly, are pink. In the right light, on a clean goose, they are a joyous bubblegum pink, though this too changes, with mud, light and even with tired eyes which have spent hours peering down a scope. I saw none today but a tiny, fickle fraction of pinkfeet have orange legs. There could have been orange-footed pink-footed geese in today's flock but their legs were hardly on view, as they rested and fed in the tall maize stubble of the field. I could see their faces though, especially once the bulk of the flock had slowly worked across the field towards me. Many times I saw birds with a narrow fringe of white round the base of the bill, the commonest variant plumage that we see. As geese came and went in their thousands, through my long watch here, the other unusual pinkfoot that I saw was a single leucistic bird, like the one that Mark and Lynnette saw southwest of the park at the start of the month. This is a variant that we less commonly see, a lovely mushroom-coloured goose with a somewhat darker, cinnamon neck.

These huge flocks are where rarer geese can be found, by sifting through the countless pinkfeet, panning meditatively with a telescope, hour by hour and goose by goose. The first two that I found today – separately, and thousands of geese apart from one another – were both of a common species, yet strangely also rare visitors, perhaps. They were greylags. The greylag, as discussed last month, is now a very common breeding bird in Norfolk, thanks to deliberate introductions in the twentieth century. Much further north, in the Hebrides and Iceland, it remains a true wild bird. Even before the species' reintroduction here, northern greylags would sometimes appear in Norfolk's winter flocks of pinkfeet. It is tempting, seeing single greylags behaving naturally among vast pinkfoot flocks, to wonder whether they too might be wanderers from Iceland, caught up in this great migrant throng.

The Meaning of Geese

There were other scarce geese among today's pinkfeet, and some of them could only have been wild. I caught the next two in my scope as they flew to land among thousands of pinks. With white blazes and mottled bellies, they were an adult pair of Russian white-fronted geese. Whitefronts are around the same size and shape as pinkfeet, but their slender, pale pink bills afford them a more distinguished look. Their legs, though I could not see them today, are the bright orange of an over-boiled carrot, and their plumage is uniformly grey-brown, without a pinkfoot's watercolour washes. The whitefront's slightly paler belly is heavily marked with black bars and blotches. It is a handsome goose and these two, to my delight, were the first of my winter with geese.

Two small flocks of Russian whitefronts are faithful to ancestral wintering sites in Norfolk. A few hundred winter in the Broads, largely in the valleys of the Yare and Thurne. Between Holkham and Burnham Overy, on the North Norfolk coast, a second flock has wintered for as long as anyone remembers. I saw my first in winter 1987, standing with our biology teacher at the top of Bone's Drift, looking north to Holkham Marsh. As we watched these beautiful geese, a female hen harrier flew over them to the west, also my very first.

Every winter, a few lost Russian whitefronts join our pinkfeet hordes, especially when hard weather pushes them off the Continent. Much later today I found a single juvenile in the flock. This was a more subtle bird, with neither its parents' rounded white blaze nor the speckled belly. A young Russian whitefront has an all-pink bill, and a meek look bestowed by the plainness of its face.

The next scarce goose I found among these thousands of pinks was far from meek. The tundra bean goose breeds

October

widely across northern Russia, and winters commonly in Europe. In the UK we are at the edge of its winter range and just a few birds occur here, typically in flocks of pinkfeet or whitefronts. Tundra beans look to me like haughty pinkfeet, an impression given by their massive, deep-based bills and the snarling crease between their upper and lower mandibles. They seem heftier than pinks, with thicker necks and more angular heads. Apart from the white vent and dark flight feathers shared by all grey geese, the plumage of the tundra bean goose is uniform grey-brown, even on the back and wings, with none of the pinkfoot's subtly blended blues and greys. A tundra bean's bill spot and legs are orange, though a more pumpkin orange, it seems to me, than a whitefront's plastic knickknack orange legs.

I saw several barnacle geese too. The first seven – a pair, and shortly afterwards a family, I assumed, of five – all flew right over the field, choosing not to stop, despite hundreds of pinkfeet coming and going throughout the day. Barnacle geese are lovely things and seeing them is always a joy, but their origins, like the greylags', are complex. The world-famous Svalbard population, beloved of documentaries, winters on the Solway, notably at the Wildfowl and Wetlands Trust's Caerlaverock reserve. Greenland-breeding birds winter principally on Islay and in Ireland. Increasingly, Kane tells me, some of these Greenland birds migrate no further north than Iceland, staying there to breed. When Peter Scott and his colleagues visited Iceland in 1951 they found a single lost barnacle goose which, not finding a partner of its own species, had paired with a pink-footed goose. Their hybrid eggs were lost to predators. Around 1,000 pairs of barnacles now nest in Iceland, Kane says.

The Meaning of Geese

A third population of barnacle geese nests in western Siberia and here the story becomes more tortuous still. Over the past fifty years, birds from this Siberian population, which winters in Germany and the Netherlands, have increasingly stayed to breed at traditional stopover sites in the Baltic – in Sweden, Estonia, Finland, and Denmark – much as many Greenland birds now go no further than Iceland. Extraordinarily, some birds from the same population now stay in the Netherlands to breed, forming large colonies on islands in inland rivers. Though some ornithologists believe this behavioural change reflects interbreeding with escaped birds from captivity, this Arctic goose appears to be in the process of becoming temperate.

It is not unreasonable to assume that some Iceland-breeding barnacles get caught up in flocks of pink-footed geese and carried with them to Norfolk. Nor is it impossible that Siberian birds wintering in the Netherlands hop across here, and this especially seems possible in midwinter, when cold snaps see tundra bean geese, Russian whitefronts and barnacles from the Continent appear in our pinkfoot flocks.

The fly in the ointment of my barnacles' credentials is that there is now a colony of barnacle geese on Holkham Lake, just three miles from where I was watching today's wild flock of geese. The first pair, Andy tells me, nested on the lake in 2004. This year around thirty-five pairs nested and his highest count was 330 birds. Curiously, each year, having bred, the Holkham birds disappear for several months, seeming to undertake migration. Just over two months ago, in sunny August, I saw a large flock over Cley, right at the time when Andy observed they had left the lake at Holkham. Where our Norfolk breeders go in winter no one yet knows.

October

Against this background, today's seven barnacles south of Wells were a mystery. With the flock gone from Holkham, it is unlikely that they were local breeding birds. Were they then birds from Iceland or even Greenland? Were they birds from Siberia, or Siberian birds which had nested as nearby as the Netherlands? Or were they feral birds, of captive origin, from somewhere nearby which just fancied a day out with the pinkfeet?

Whatever their credentials, they were beautiful. A barnacle goose's lustrous black neck embraces its pure white face, like a gloved hand holding a ball. Its black eyes and neat black bill are joined by a short black line, giving it a look of mild reproach. Its body is a soft pale grey, barred lightly on the flanks in darker grey and heavily on the back in black. It is hard to look at a barnacle goose and not feel happy.

These seven were not the only barnacles I saw today. The last was found by my friend Nick Parsons. I'd been staring through my scope for five hours, wholly lost in the lives of geese, when a voice right behind me spoke my name. 'Sorry,' the voice continued when I jumped, 'I didn't mean to startle you.' Nick has been watching this enthralling flock for two days now, and together we continued working through it. First I found another adult Russian whitefront, resting with hundreds of pinkfeet in the cereal field to the west. Then Nick found another barnacle, standing alone at the front of the feeding pinks, walking around as though lost.

I asked him how many birds he thought were gathered here. 'Ten thousand at least,' he said, 'maybe fifteen.' I don't see the world in numbers. I'm not the man to ask to count a flock of geese, but all day, whenever I felt sure that all North

The Meaning of Geese

Norfolk's pinkfeet must be here, hundreds and hundreds more would arrive to join the flock. All day I was transported: to a place of focus and of stillness, amid the din and Arctic energy of it all.

This evening Nick texted some photos he has taken with James McCallum in the past two days. Even after six hours watching geese today, I told him his photos thrilled me. 'You're a fellow sufferer.' He answered wryly. 'Good.'

NOVEMBER

wild, empty spaces

As brent flocks gather on the coast, and huge flocks of pinkfeet roam North Norfolk, I speak to ornithologist friends around the world about their lives with geese. In harvested fields of sugar beet, tensions mount between pinkfeet and farmers who are keen to sow winter cereals. In a brent flock I meet winter's first black brant, a visitor from the Pacific.

Monday 2nd November

Kane is not the only Englishman to have followed Peter Scott's path north to the breeding grounds of the pink-footed goose. In September a friend put me in touch with artist Jonathan Yule whose work captures pinkfeet both in Norfolk and in Iceland. Jonathan's first email was warm and encouraging, full of enthusiasm for geese and for my own journey with them. We arranged to meet by Zoom and spoke at length, a conversation infused with Jonathan's long love of wild places, and his passion for geese. Afterwards he generously sent a copy of his book *Under a Colour-Washed Sky* which tells the story, in words and watercolours, of a life spent with livestock, with landscape and with geese. It is beautiful, the more so for a delicate pencil sketch of pinkfeet landing which he drew for me inside the cover.

Geese have flocked to Jonathan's life for as long as he remembers. It was brents he loved first, growing up in the Colne and Blackwater estuaries of Essex, and later studying agriculture there. He writes of dark-bellied brent geese in his book: 'Once I had learnt that they breed and summer on the tundra of the Taymyr peninsula and Novaya Zemlya, alongside polar bears, Arctic foxes, snowy owls and a multitude of other species that spend the breeding season in that remote wilderness, the spell was cast.'

Pinkfeet came into his life when he moved to Norfolk, invited by friends to work on a Breckland farm which they had bought. For years he was a shepherd, running sheep both on Brecks grassland on the Stanford Training Area and on sugar beet up by the coast between Brancaster and Docking. Here, on this North Norfolk farm, pink-footed geese were as closely his companions as his dogs and sheep. At night he would paint the Norfolk scenes that he had witnessed in the day, and dream of painting for a living.

Jonathan became a full-time artist – with the safety net of some contract shepherding – after a meeting with Peter Scott. Reasoning that 'if you don't ask you don't get' he wrote to his artist hero, describing his work and his relationship with wildfowl. The great conservationist's PA replied, inviting him to Slimbridge. 'I cannot explain how elated and at the same time terrified I was. So, a few weeks later, I drove down to Gloucestershire with 12 watercolours in a folder at my side.'

Even forty years after the encounter Jonathan's face lit up as he told me how supportive Peter Scott had been, studying his early paintings with care. 'He enthused where he could and criticised gently where he felt that he had to, but constructively.' Looking at length at a painting of Bewick's swans in flight over a flooded meadow at East Wretham, Scott commented that he wished he too could paint such skies, avowing himself unable to paint in watercolour. He praised Jonathan's affinity with landscape, urging him never to lose it.

'He had given up a great deal of his time, and could potentially have killed my confidence there and then had he not been so sensitive and empathetic. He was gracious and kind, and I will forever be grateful to him. That was the day when I made up my mind to concentrate on my painting.'

Later, now a professional artist, Jonathan stood at Ken Hill in West Norfolk with his friend Dr Michael Petch, watching pinkfeet. As they watched, Jonathan recalls in his book, 'Michael expressed his desire to visit Iceland and see the geese on their breeding grounds. This was also a long-held dream of mine.' After making enquiries of Dr Tony Fox, who worked at Slimbridge for the Wildfowl Trust, the pair were introduced to Icelandic farmers Einar Jonsson and Anna Halldorsdottir.

Thus for thirty years, without a break until this Covid year, Jonathan has visited the Icelandic tundra, his farming friends, and his beloved pinkfeet. Michael Petch has almost always accompanied him. Son of Charles Petch, first author of the 1968 *Flora of Norfolk*, he has brought a love of tundra flowers to their goose-watching adventures.

At the heart of their Icelandic sojourns is Anna, owner of the farm since her husband died many years ago, mother of a family and dear friend to Jonathan and Michael. Anna drives them up to the valleys every day, and they walk home. She is amused by their excitement on seeing the first geese on her farm each year; some of them surely the same birds which left Norfolk just a few short weeks before. 'The geese are actually a menace to her in many ways,' Jonathan writes. 'Her precious fields of grass in the valleys, from which she makes winter feed silage for the winter-housed sheep, are fallen upon by hungry geese fresh from their journey from the UK. Sometimes in early spring, the fields are grey with geese. Happily, they soon disperse to their favoured breeding areas higher up the valley, and leave Anna and her grass in peace.'

'Icelanders,' Jonathan chuckled as he told me, 'think we're completely bonkers. They see the geese as being like rabbits, a plague. Plus we walk everywhere. Icelanders never walk anywhere.' Some of Jonathan and Michael's walking in fact means crawling on their bellies, as they learned early on how exquisitely wary the geese are in the valley wetlands where they feed with their young. 'In the first couple of years we would walk over the ridges into the valleys,' he told me. 'But the geese see you in a second. The sentries are on it and as soon as they see you the families run away. Literally the valleys will empty.'

'Now we know, and our approach is similar to stalking in the Highlands. We crawl from rock to rock, using gullies to remain hidden, and then scan the valley from our vantage point. The reward is a charming spectacle of grazing family parties, bathing, preening or simply resting in the brittle sunshine. We then slide away, unseen, and leave them in peace.'

For thirty years they have watched the lives of geese in these high Icelandic valleys. They have many times observed geese killed by predators too: Arctic skuas taking goslings, and gyrfalcons, Arctic foxes and great skuas all taking adults. When I expressed surprise that great skuas could manage adult geese, Jonathan described two skuas harrying a flightless moulting flock on a lagoon by a moraine. Eventually they grabbed a hapless adult goose by the wing.

'I love wild, empty places,' he told me, 'and Iceland has them in bucketloads.' It is this same wildness which draws him, time and again, to the marshes of the Norfolk coast, and their geese. When we spoke, he had just been up to sail with Mike, to watch geese making landfall, reaching their winter home. 'When I see pinkfeet come in from the sea' he said, 'and they call as they see Burnham Norton or Holkham, it makes me well up with the joy of it all. It's not just a noise. It means: I'm here. It's the unbreakable thread.'

Thursday 5th November

The feeding behaviour of our pinkfeet visitors is changing fast. They're spreading across harvested fields of sugar beet, often out of range of my bike and my legs. New pinkfeet are still flooding into Norfolk, raising the possibility that rarer geese will come here with them. Yesterday two friends in Yorkshire texted news of pinkfeet heading south over their heads, and colleagues elsewhere in Yorkshire and Northumberland have said the same on social media. A couple of days ago Andy sent news that the roosts around Holkham and Wells had risen to 29,000 birds.

I cycled north again this morning, to the maize field south of Wells where the massive flock of pinkfeet and other geese has been feeding these past few days. Autumn's drizzle has cleared at last and the temperature has sharply

The Meaning of Geese

dropped. The first frosts are here; and with them, bright mornings of lingering mist, and cold knuckles on the handlebars of my bike.

Only a fraction of last week's geese remained in the field today, feeding far more busily than before. Throughout the time I watched, small groups of geese passed over, circling above the field as if wishing to land, but flying on. A few came down, but very few. The field's bounty, it would seem, is spent. Time now for the geese to feed elsewhere across the Norfolk landscape. A buzzard and a kite were crouched on the muddy ground, picking at something I couldn't see. Ash later told me he had seen a pinkfoot lying dead there.

Grey partridges gave their rasping calls in the next-door field, and a hare ran the length of the stubble rows towards me, unaware of the huddled figure in the hedge, hooded against the cold. I scanned the pinks from side to side, as always, to see what they were doing and whether any scarcer geese were with them. All the birds today were pinkfeet, but far to the back of the field, against the hedge, I spotted a goose with a Darvic collar, an adult with its partner and their two young of this year. I could make out that the collar was silver, but the bird was much too far away to read the code for Kane. When a Holkham gamekeeper trundled on his quad bike into view, the game was up: all two thousand geese before me noisily took flight. I stood by the empty field of mud and faded maize stalks, and decided to follow the panicked birds, down to the coast at Holkham.

The geese along Lady Anne's Drive were feeding too, ripping at grasses with pink-blotched bills, powered by muscled necks. Among them there were wigeon, the handsome males

November

moulting into butter-fronted breeding plumage, and a single family of dark-bellied brents.

I searched for other strangers, stopping at a brown shape in the grass. It was a hare, waving its black-edged ears as it too grazed. Side by side today I have seen these two adaptable herbivores – goose and hare – both in a muddy maize field and a grazing marsh.

Sunday 8th November

Two days ago my good friend David Stubbs texted a short film showing 360 greylag geese heading out to feed from their roost on the lake at Raynham Hall. West Raynham is just three villages upriver from my home; so this morning I left on my bike in the early mist to join David for a walk. The first geese we saw together were not greylags, but a pair of Egyptian geese, among the stately lime trees of the park. 'It's time I wrote about Egyptian geese, isn't it?' I said to David, with a sigh. He nodded in assent.

Egyptian geese are strange, misshapen things. Broadly goose-shaped, they are badly goose shaped, with none of the wild poise of a whitefront or a brent. Their rubbery pink legs, perfect for perching in the trees in which they nest, look too long for their bodies, and their blunt pink bills seem somehow sullied. Around their defiant yellow eyes there is a stain of chestnut brown, too blotchy to be called a mask. It is only in flight that these odd birds look beautiful, as their wings are patterned strikingly in black, chestnut, white and shot silk green. Alas, whenever an Egyptian goose is flying it is likely also to be shouting. The simplest, and most palatable, of the sounds it makes is a breathless hiss; but as an Egyptian goose grows more excited – and an Egyptian goose is very

The Meaning of Geese

excitable indeed – it breaks into a raucous jackass laugh. Even in Africa, where they belong, these birds are always noisy and aggressive.

For two months I have been putting off Egyptian geese, for the simple reason that they make things complex. I like Egyptian geese well enough. I have known them in North Norfolk my whole life long, and I would miss them if they were not here, but they don't fit comfortably into my story of geese.

For a start, they are not geese, though they look more or less like geese, behave in many ways like geese, are the size of geese and are known as geese. Much as, in our age of DNA sequencing, taxonomy is a fluid subject, Northern Hemisphere true geese – including all the species we have met so far – are typically placed in two genera. The genus, in the plural genera, is the level of taxonomic hierarchy, and therefore closeness of relationship, one step higher than species, which is represented in the first word of a species' scientific name. The second word, never capitalised, refers to the species. Thus the greylag is *Anser anser*.

This genus *Anser* includes all of the grey geese – greylag, white-fronted, lesser white-fronted, pink-footed, tundra bean and taiga bean – the two white geese – Ross's and snow – and three Asian or Pacific geese which don't quite fit into those categories – bar-headed, emperor and swan geese. The genus *Branta* includes the generally smaller, darker Northern Hemisphere geese – barnacle, red-breasted, brent, cackling and Canada – though some regional forms of Canada geese are very large indeed, including those introduced to the UK. Also in the genus *Branta* is the curious nēnē or Hawaiian goose. Together with the two genera of swans and the strange Cape Barren goose of southern Australia,

November

Anser and *Branta* make up the subfamily Anserinae of the waterfowl family Anatidae.

The six species of shelduck (plus a seventh which has almost certainly become extinct in living memory) are in a separate subfamily the Tadorninae, which takes its name from the genus in which most of them are placed: *Tadorna*. Shelducks, despite approaching geese in size, are definitely duck-shaped, so we happily embrace them as ducks in the English language. Now things start to get a little complex. In the temperate regions of the Southern Hemisphere, the ecological niche of true geese (essentially ripping grass and other short vegetation while walking on land near water) is occupied by the sheldgeese. These – and the clue is in the name – are genetically shelducks though in structure and behaviour they are remarkably similar to geese. In South America there are six species, traditionally placed in two genera, though recent genetic analysis has rearranged them. In the highlands of Ethiopia, just north of the Equator, the very beautiful blue-winged goose looks for all the world like a sheldgoose, but its DNA calls this affinity into question and it is no longer counted as one. Several aberrant ducks do, however, belong in the Tadorninae. The final member – resplendent in a genus of its own: *Alopochen* – is our very own Egyptian goose.

The name Egyptian is a misnomer too. Or rather a huge simplification. Egyptian geese do occur in Egypt, but they are also found right across Africa south of the Sahara, wherever there are wetlands in open country, as far south as the Cape of Good Hope. No hippo wallow in Tanzania or crocodile pool in the Okavango is complete without Egyptian geese.

So how did these confounding birds come to be by a cold lake in North Norfolk in November, where I saw them today?

The Meaning of Geese

Nobody is sure, though Egyptian geese were first recorded in British captive collections in the seventeenth century. Some sources suggest that the Egyptian goose was established in small numbers as a wild breeding bird in the UK by the eighteenth century.

For decades, indeed perhaps two centuries, the UK population of the Egyptian goose – essentially by the late twentieth century equivalent to its Norfolk population – grew only very slowly. In the 1999 *Birds of Norfolk*, Bill Sutherland suggests that the Egyptian goose's low productivity in Norfolk might result from its nesting very early in the year and the consequent vulnerability of chicks to winter cold.

In the twenty years since *Birds of Norfolk* was published, the Norfolk population of Egyptian geese has risen sharply and has spilled into other areas of England. As a young birder I would see Egyptian geese only around Holkham; now they are common anywhere there is freshwater in the county and frequently I hear them flying past my house. In the 1990s the UK population numbered around 800 birds. The British Trust for Ornithology now estimates a winter population of 5,600 birds, with 1,850 pairs breeding. This represents a sevenfold increase in population in twenty years. As our climate changes and our springs come ever earlier, perhaps Egyptian geese simply fledge more chicks in the UK now than they could just twenty years ago.

There was plenty of other wildlife on my walk with David today. We spooked a hind and her well-grown calf in a patch of alder by the Wensum and we heard a water rail screeching from the river's reed. As I counted greylags in a field, a flock of crossbills fussed around distant hilltop conifers. There was a kingfisher and there were teal and gadwall on the lake. But it was Egyptian geese which stayed with me.

November

Tuesday 10th November

I learned yesterday from my friend Tim Stowe that the Wells Harbour brent geese have begun to feed on the short grass north of the football pitch, as every winter they do. This morning I cycled through the lurking mist to Wells, where I met Tim on the quay. A grey wagtail bounded over, as I chained my bike, cutting the gloom with its knife-sharp call, and a starling on the harbour office piped in perfect imitation of a teal.

Some 300 dark-bellied brent geese were feeding in the field, plucking at grass with their stout black bills. Most were adults, though a few families with young were on the near edge of the flock. We quickly found a striking bird among them: a first-generation black brant hybrid. Patterned like a brant, this bird had the flat grey mantle of a dark-bellied brent, a mere shade darker than the feeding geese around it. Here, amazingly, was a bird bearing genes from both extremes of the Russian Arctic.

A dog off its leash put the brents off the field, so Tim and I walked north along the seawall, past two greenshanks in the harbour channel and a kingfisher, whirring above the frigid water. As we went, we talked of geese. Tim, like Jonathan Yule, grew up in Essex, watching dark-bellied brents in coastal marshes. From Cambridge, where he studied in the 1970s, he and a friend would drive a clapped-out car across the country in search of birds. In the days before books showed geese in flight, or explained where each species could best be found, they twice drove to Northumberland looking for Russian whitefronts. 'We didn't know then – because we would have come here – that whitefronts wintered in Norfolk.'

The Meaning of Geese

From Northumberland, they crossed the north of England to the Solway, and Caerlaverock, to immerse themselves in Svalbard barnacle geese. They drove on to the Ken-Dee marshes, where a flock of Greenland white-fronted geese could be found in winter, as they still can to this day. On 2nd November 1975, Tim got his first speeding ticket. He and his friend were hurtling back from Essex, having seen their first red-breasted goose in a coastal flock of dark-bellied brents. The ticket rankles with him to this day.

Tim is a lover of geese, for whom – despite an ecology PhD and a life spent translating science into conservation policy – geese are far more than simply winter birds. 'There's something free-spirited and mystical about them,' he said to me today. 'I don't know where that came from. My early days of birdwatching were largely on my own. There was certainly nobody showing me geese and saying: isn't that fantastic?'

A group of brents flew over the seawall, low above our heads, murmuring sagely as they do. 'I love that noise,' I said, essentially to myself. 'It's great,' said Tim. 'It's something I associate with my early birdwatching days. Brent chatter is like some rolling mechanical sound. Have you ever heard a cement mixer being cleaned with bricks?'

We ambled back. Spread out in groups across the harbour saltmarsh, our 300 brents could still be seen. 'To people who've been brought up in this landscape,' Tim mused aloud, 'they're integral to it. If you ever came out and they weren't there, you'd know that something was wrong.' It's true. Our winter marshes would be desolate without these untamed beings of the north.

Tim said goodbye and, as I fumbled with my bike chain, a kite flapped low across the harbour. As one, 300 brents took flight. Filling the town with Russian conversation, they dropped to the sweet grass of the field they'll graze all winter. I cycled south and home.

Saturday 14th November

At the start of 1997, I fled from Oxford and my MSc, and took a break which lasted more than two years. For the first few months I came home to Norfolk, where, birding with Gav along the coast, I met a lanky Dutchman, Kell Eradus.

Though Kell and his British wife Alison moved back to the Netherlands years ago, and I have since spent many years abroad, we have remained close friends. Ours is an easy friendship, enriched by shared experience and values, which springs to life whenever we hear from one another. In the middle of our two-hour conversation on Zoom last night I blurted how much I'd missed them both. Kell's face lit up with a goofy smile, 'I've missed you too.'

We were talking about geese. For years Kell was a gooseringer, working with the Netherlands' greylag specialist Berend Voslamber. Sometimes Alison supported them, helping to round up moulting flocks, and she has often reflected Kell's geese in her art. A linocut of his favourite greylag, a young male with a green neck collar numbered Z38, was hanging on the wall behind them as we spoke.

'Do people in the UK still hate greylags?' Kell began, in his bull-by-the-horns way. 'I think they're the best.' Whereas in England greylags were deliberately introduced by wildfowlers as quarry and are disdained by birders, in the Netherlands the greylag population has largely arisen from the natural ebb and flow of birds from different parts of Europe. The great majority, Kell is adamant, are of pure wild origin. They have simply chosen not to migrate from the Netherlands, and have stayed to breed; these days in great numbers.

From the 1960s to the 1980s a large moulting roost of greylags visited the Oostvaardersplassen, a huge rewilding project close to Amsterdam. The birds came from East Germany and possibly as far as Poland. 'They don't come any more,' Kell explained with animation, 'because there is no space for them. The place is already full of resident greylags.' It is these Dutch-breeding birds which most excite him.

'In the years that I worked with Berend,' he said, 'I realised that all the hours I spent with geese only gave me more questions than answers.' Each year the team observed that female geese, which had grazed all winter long on nitrogen-enriched commercial grassland, would move in early spring – just before they laid – into natural grassland, with a greater diversity of plants. Berend surmised that the females needed nutrients from specific plants to lay their eggs; but chemical analysis of the flora has shed no light on what these critical nutrients are.

Likewise, year after year, the team watched as parent greylags led their families through a predictable series of grazing spots as the goslings grew. It seemed the adults were guiding their young to the minerals needed for each stage of growth, but again conclusive evidence has yet to be found.

In greylags, Canada geese and barnacles, Berend's team has also witnessed older siblings – chicks from the previous year – joining their parents in raising goslings, gaining parental experience themselves and lending their vigilant eyes to the care of the young. The presence of extra adults translates into safer feeding for the chicks.

November

Most remarkably of all, the team has witnessed greylag parents encouraging their young to join the broods of the most successful local pairs. 'I've seen it in real life.' Kell's voice became insistent as he explained. 'In a breeding population you have very successful pairs, which raise young almost every year. They are a tiny fraction of the population. Less successful pairs deliberately bring their young near very successful pairs and persuade them to switch broods. It works for both pairs. The less successful birds pass their young to more successful birds to be raised, and the more successful birds' chicks are statistically less likely to be taken by predators.'

For as long as Kell and I have been friends, he's hurled himself headlong into the study and conservation of wildlife. These days he belongs to an international group which breeds threatened Central American livebearing fish, some of which are now extinct in the wild. The fish, their tanks and the outdoor ponds in which they spend the summer, loom large in the life that he shares with Alison and their two grown-up children.

But I sensed that this passion for fish was not all that had torn Kell from his love of geese. I asked why he gave up ringing and studying them. Kell leaned back in his spoke-backed chair and replied, 'Because of the politics surrounding killing greylags.' On account of perceived impacts on farming, tens of thousands of greylags are shot in the Netherlands every year, or rounded up and gassed. The team, Kell felt, was put under pressure to justify culling these intelligent, long-lived birds. 'Maybe I'm a sensitive little bird myself,' my dear friend said, with a flickering smile. 'They're partners for life, these geese; an example of how we should stay together ourselves.'

The greylags – as a population, at least – seem always to have the last laugh. At the height of the culling years, entire colonies of eggs were destroyed. The following year not a single nest would be found; for the geese had moved deep into cover for safety. 'They learned,' Kell said. 'They were hiding their nests.' And at sites where huge numbers of resident geese had been gassed, their place was taken by incoming birds, keen to cash in on perfect conditions for rearing young.

'Geese are very adaptable birds.' Kell said last night, his eyes alight with love for them. 'They surprise you over and over.'

Sunday 15th November

I put Kane in touch with Andy this week, so together they can plan to ring moulting barnacle geese at Holkham in July next year. When Andy took me onto the marsh in August, the barnacle geese had just left Holkham, and he was itching to find out where they went in winter. By chance Kane told me recently that he and a friend were studying English-breeding barnacles and were looking for new colonies to ring. Were birds moving between colonies in England, they wondered. Were they joining wild flocks of Siberian geese on the continent, in winter, or indeed to breed?

Questions about Norfolk's breeding barnacle geese were in my mind as I spoke to Kell and Alison two nights ago. Tens of thousands of pairs of barnacle geese now nest in the Netherlands. Most of them, Kell insists, are wild birds from the Siberian population which has spread southwest through the Baltic. There are records of the same ringed birds nesting in the Netherlands and the Baltic in consecutive years. 'The risks of migration,' Kell believes, 'are now greater than the benefits. There's more snow on the ground in their breeding sites these days, so they can't feed when they arrive.' In consequence, the Dutch population of barnacle geese has risen steeply. Like greylags, they now pose a threat to farmers' crops and are culled in their thousands each year.

In his goose-ringing days Kell became adept at catching female barnacle geese at their colonies along Dutch rivers. He would flush the goose from her nest and set up a net beside it. When she returned and had settled to sit, he would drop the trap with a tug on a string from where he lay hidden nearby. He also took part in the ringing of flightless, moulting birds, herding them into pens as Kane does with pinkfeet in Iceland and proposes to do with barnacles in Holkham Park next year.

Barnacle geese are not only more numerous as breeding birds in the Netherlands now. Wintering birds occur in ever greater numbers too, and over larger areas of the country. Intriguingly, the spread of winter flocks of barnacle geese has pushed the country's 500,000 wintering Russian white-fronted geese to the south. 'We have more and more winter barnacles,' Kell said. 'First they were on islands off the coast, then in the north, then in the west. They keep the grassland very short, so there is no food for whitefronts. They basically kick the whitefronts out.'

Perversely, at the same time, the Russian white-fronted goose has become a Dutch breeding bird. This wildest goose of the Arctic tundra has – almost unthinkably – settled to breed in the temperate wetlands of the Netherlands. Initially, a few birds injured by hunters failed to leave on migration. Their partners – their pair bond too strong for them to leave – stayed too. They tried to breed but, for the first few years, all their young were lost to temperate parasites, not known in the clean, cold tundra of the Arctic. Somehow, over time, the goslings of these stranded whitefronts developed resistance and survived. Today, to everyone's amazement, up to 700 pairs of Russian whitefronts breed in the Netherlands.

Still one more goose has recently joined the breeding fauna of the Netherlands. The bar-headed goose nests in Asia's bleakest uplands, both in the Himalayas and Hindu Kush, and in western Mongolia's Gobi-Altai. It winters largely in South and Southeast Asia. Countless times I have seen this stunning bird in India or with demoiselle cranes on the shore of Khar Us Lake, outside Mongolia's far western city of Khovd.

In shape and stature, bar-headed geese are clearly like the pinkfeet, greylags and whitefronts that I have seen this autumn; but these gorgeous birds are patterned like no other member of the genus. They are paler by far than other grey geese: a silver grey, pencilled with chalky white. In their throats, up the back of their necks, and at the rear of their flanks, this colour is touched by a steelier grey, rusting to brown. Their faces are white and a line of white cuts down each side of the neck, between the darkness of the throat and nape. A band of black wraps round the head, from the rear of each neat back eye. Beneath it, at the top of the slender neck, sits a second, shorter black band. A buttercup yellow bill, which is tipped in black, and bold orange legs complete this stylish goose. It is the barhead's voice, though, which takes me straight to the jheels of Bharatpur on a misty winter morning or to the silty vastness of the Brahmaputra. Bar-headed geese give a sorrowful, buzzing honk, quite different from the nasal cackle of the pink-billed eastern greylags with which I have almost always seen them.

A bird as handsome as a barhead is prized by captive breeders. Both in the UK and elsewhere, some young birds escape and settle with greylags or Canada geese. Sometimes they form mixed-species pairs, but with luck they may encounter other barheads and try to breed. In this way a tiny population of bar-headed geese has formed in the Netherlands. There are fewer than ninety pairs, Kell says, but he feels that bar-headed geese are in his country to stay.

Having written these words this evening, I have learned, in a message from India, that an old birding friend from Bharatpur has died. A wise birder and a kindly man, for decades he watched as autumn's geese and ducks flocked to his wetland home. Next spring, I fondly think, he will fly to Mount Kailash with the bar-headed geese when they go; and there at the feet of Lord Shiva he will rest.

Monday 16th November

Behind my little flint house the Wensum flows. Rising a few miles west of here, this lovely chalk river bisects mid-Norfolk, then crosses Norwich. Southeast of the city it is joined from the west by the River Yare. Though the Wensum is the larger river, together the two continue as the Yare, winding east to Breydon Water, where they mix with all the rivers of the Broads, and bleed to sea through the historic port of Great Yarmouth.

In 1912 a group of Dutch investors built the UK's first sugar beet factory, beside the Yare at Cantley, overlooking a

The Meaning of Geese

site now managed by the RSPB for wildlife. These marshes are visited by thousands of birds each winter, among them pinkfeet, whitefronts, wigeon, teal and starlings, and their attendant peregrines. Since at least the 1920s, and probably far longer, this stretch of marshes by the Yare has held one of the UK's only two winter flocks of taiga bean geese. The other flock visits the Slamannan Plateau in Falkirk. Whereas a tundra bean goose is thick-necked and stocky, a taiga bean has a swan-like grace, bestowed by its slender bill and its greatly longer neck. The UK flocks of this elegant bird breed in central Scandinavia and belong to a European population in steep decline. In consequence, and also thanks to climate change offering better winter feeding on the Continent, the Norfolk flock of taiga bean geese has dwindled almost to nothing in my lifetime. Where once 400 geese could be expected in the winter marshes of the Yare, last year fewer than half a dozen came. Taiga beans are always slow to arrive, but so far this winter not a single bird has been seen.

The inevitable loss of taiga bean geese from the Yare will weigh on those of us who know and love them, for whom the natural tapestry of Norfolk will be one stitch less wild. Oddly, though, the building of Cantley beet factory, next to their ancestral marshes, set in train events which would hugely favour the global population of pink-footed geese. Following the factory's completion, sugar beet rapidly became a favoured crop of UK lowland farmers and during the 1920s a further seventeen factories were built. The passing of the Sugar Industry Act in 1936 created the British Sugar Corporation, to manage the nation's sugar factories and production. Today – my friend Harry Mitchell of British Sugar

November

tells me – sugar is grown in Norfolk, Suffolk, Cambridgeshire, Lincolnshire and the south of Yorkshire, and is processed in just four streamlined factories: Newark, Wissington, Bury St Edmunds and Cantley.

As I learned from my distant cousin David Lyles last month, with the advent of mechanical harvesters, which top beet in the field, beet leftovers became available to wildlife, including pink-footed geese. In the 1970s the resourceful geese began to fly inland to glean these nutritious tops. Of the UK's pinkfeet (which represent virtually all the breeding birds of Iceland and Greenland) many stay all winter in Lancashire or eastern Scotland, where they forage both in grassland and in harvested crops of carrots and potatoes. Most of the rest come to Norfolk, for December and January at least, where sugar beet has featured prominently in their diet throughout my life. When we spoke in mid-September, Kane told me that UK agriculture, including Norfolk sugar beet, had been a significant driver of the huge increase in the Iceland pinkfoot population.

On Friday night Nick Parsons texted with news of 5,000 pinks foraging in a large field of harvested beet just west of North Creake. All weekend it has poured, so I have stayed at home and read; but this morning I packed my panniers and cycled through the lingering drizzle, lured by the promise of a brighter day. It was cold as I went, the raw cold of a keen wind after two days of rain. Whichever way the road turned I seemed to be heading into the wind and, by the time I reached the hill which rises west from the Jolly Farmers pub, my legs were suffering. Halfway up the hill, as I dropped a gear, I heard the thrilling talk of pinkfeet. I thanked Nick out loud and laboured on.

The Meaning of Geese

At the gate of the field was a silver van, meaning Ash Saunders was here and watching geese already. I found him sheltering against the winter-blackened hedge, in gloves, a thick coat and a woolly hat. Around his feet were red deer slots, left by the sugar-scavenging night shift, and ahead of him, across the muddy field, thousands of geese.

I quickly found the adult greylag he had seen. Soon we also saw a single Russian whitefront, a young bird of the year. Otherwise, all the thousands of geese we watched today were pinkfeet. Muddy pinkfeet at that, their faces coated with a slip of clay, leaving them beige-billed in this morning's gloomy light.

Among these countless birds, Ash found a pinkfoot with a silver collar, bearing the letters VVA. I texted Kane and quickly he replied with the bird's life story. Ringed in Iceland as an adult male in July 2017, it was seen in December of the same year at Cresswell in Northumberland. The following year, early in October, it was at Loch Leven in Perth and Kinross, and in January 2019 it was seen again at Cresswell. Before today it had never been reported from Norfolk.

Intellectually, I understand that pinkfeet come to us from Iceland – I have thought of almost nothing but geese for three months now – but the knowledge that, while he moulted in summer 2017, this bird was herded to a pen there; that he was gently measured, ringed and collared; that he has since been seen three times in the north of the UK; this knowledge makes this goose a thread which binds each of us observers to his story; and to the great flow of muscles, feather, genes and shrill, cloud-piercing cries from the northern tundra to Norfolk's mud and back in spring again.

November

Tuesday 17th November

This was a day of geese and of landscape. A day of seeing a little further into their world, and the demands of their existence. Of beginning to think like a goose.

It began last night with a text from Ash with the news that in the last of the light Nick Parsons had found a huge pinkfoot flock feeding in harvested maize just north of Great Walsingham. We agreed to meet there this morning, and I cycled north at eight. Beyond Great Snoring, coasting down the hill to Little Walsingham, I saw the geese, swarming in the northeast sky.

As I emerged from the wooded valley of Great Walsingham, along the tiny Wighton Road, the pinkfeet were over fields not far to the north. The maize stubble in which the bulk of them were feeding was largely lost from view, in a glacial fold, but on either side large groups of pinks were resting on winter cereal shoots. I stopped just short of a hole in the densely ivied hedge of the field by the road, mounted my scope on its tripod, and crept to the gap. Hundreds of pinkfeet were here, most of them resting; but beyond, in the maize, past a straggly, unloved hedge, there were countless hundreds more, thousands perhaps in the valley lost to view, all of them picking at fallen grains.

These were the busiest geese I have seen this year, milling across the dry brown earth and the spun gold stubble, gleaning maize; ganders jousting at one another with outstretched necks, warm breasts glowing beneath the morning's nacreous sky. A hare loped past, a buzzard mewed, and it was happiness to lose myself among them.

Gunshots woke me from my reverie, not gas guns, which merely frighten birds, but shotguns. The geese – in their numberless thousands – took to the air in panic, swirling in stacks above the fields, filling the still cold morning with their din. Just a handful remained on the ground ahead of me. I stayed with them, while the shrieking airborne hordes spread out, deciding where to land, where they would be safe.

In time, they began returning to the nearest field, wave after wave coming down, their front flank edging ever closer, the wheat's green smothered brown and grey by landing geese. They remained alert, each bird's neck stretched, head raised like a flag, scanning for danger. Slowly, they relaxed, a bird here turning its head to preen, another lowering its bill to pluck a blade of wheat. I stood immobile, knowing much of the flock would not have landed so close had they known that I was there; but something spooked them again – more shots from two fields away perhaps – and again they took to the sky in a maelstrom of wings and noise.

Ash arrived in his van, but the rattle of linnets and breathy caw of rooks could not fill the emptiness left by the pinks. In barely half an hour I had seen a lifetime's drama among geese. Where were they now, we wondered. Had they found somewhere else to feed? Ash drove on, following news of a flock on the Wighton Road to Hindringham. I went too, on my old red bike, alone with the sky and the birds.

Ash was already turning back as I reached Wighton. Here the geese had been scared away too. Instead, he had met James McCallum painting the flock that, from different lanes, we had all seen overhead. I cycled on to say hello and found James crouched by his upturned crate, as though kneeling in prayer to the geese as he added them, stroke by meticulous stroke, to a water-washed Norfolk sky. The maize stubbles, he said, had already been drilled with wheat, and the farmer was out with his gun to scare the birds off. It made no sense – to him or to me – that these wild Icelandic pilgrims could not be granted two days' harmless feeding, in harvested beet or maize, before the fields were drilled and the flocks driven hungry away.

Ash had gone on to Cuckoo Lodge, and the maize field north of Wells where we'd watched the mighty flock at the end of last month. I took my leave of James and followed, rattling my bike along almost three miles of unmade track. There were thousands of pinks in the stubble here too; but, unlike the birds in the fresh cut maize at Great Walsingham, this flock was still. Even a marsh harrier, trailed by a young red kite, could not disturb them. 'They're using this now as a resting field,' Ash said. 'They're not being shot at here, at least.'

From time to time a group of geese would take flight and bear southwest, bound, we were sure, for the sugar beet field at Creake. We decided to regroup there. Ash drove on, but I quickly found that my goose-watching was done for the day. I had asked too much of my bike and had punctured a tyre on the track. I pumped it up and texted Ash, before limping home, stopping in each farm gate to pump again. My ruddy-darter-coloured bike and I have travelled 375 miles this autumn, in search of geese. It was surely time we had a puncture.

Wednesday 18th November

Kell's story of breeding bar-headed geese in the Netherlands took me back to the winters I've spent with these lovely birds in India. As often as not, by my side was my charismatic friend Sujan Chatterjee. Six times we have cruised together along the Brahmaputra, in Assam, from

The Meaning of Geese

Silghat to the state capital Guwahati. In winter, the river's vast silt beaches, and the wetlands of mighty Kaziranga National Park, heave with thousands of bar-headed and eastern greylag geese, ruddy shelducks, gadwall, pochard and other ducks. I love them all.

I love Sujan and his family too. Whenever I have visited Kolkata I have stayed at their welcoming home. 'How's Arpita?' I asked after his wife, when we spoke this morning on Zoom. 'She's good,' he replied in his deep, familiar voice, his Bengali diction clipped. 'She's managing two oddballs now, Torsa and me.' 'And how's Torsa?' I chuckled. Their daughter has become a young woman since I saw her last. 'She wants to be a chef!' He said, his brown eyes sparkling with amusement and pride. 'She cooks for us every day. All sorts of things. Some of her recipes take two days to prepare. It's not your regular dal sabji.'

Torsa was raised in boats and jeeps, watching tigers and Bengal floricans with her naturalist dad. Since March, as school has been closed, she has devoted her time to study, and to feeding her parents, at home. I asked of Sujan's own work as a birding guide. 'I've had time to get a lot of things sorted which I could never do on the move. The Birdwatchers' Society has grown to 110 members. We had twenty at the start of Covid. Then everybody started birding. All the IT guys are working from home. They just say when they're heading out and someone goes with them.' I asked, for accuracy's sake, whether the group that Sujan had founded was formally the West Bengal Birdwatchers Society. A laugh rose from deep in his belly. 'No! That was originally our name, but we're not allowed by the state to call ourselves West Bengal. We can't use India either. It suits us,' he continued, enjoying the irony. 'We now have members from other states, like Sikkim and

November

Assam. Even your friend Manisha in Gujarat has joined. You could be our first overseas member!' he beamed, enchanted by the notion.

Though in 2020 Sujan is confined to watching clamorous reed warblers on short walks from home, for years he has roamed all over India, sharing the country's wonderful birds with visitors and locals alike. For more than thirty years he has counted geese in West Bengal each January, as part of Wetlands International's Asian Waterbird Census.

Sujan saw his first eastern greylags many years ago, on a visit to Shantiniketan, home of Bengali icon Rabindranath Tagore, and he has since encountered vast flocks of greylags in the wetlands of Harike in Punjab. But it is bar-headed geese that he knows best; that he's seen in every chapter of their lives. Five times he's made trips through the mountains and valleys of Ladakh. Here, on the shores of Tso Moriri, Tso Kar and Pangong Tso, he has watched bar-headed pairs with their sulphur-faced chicks, alongside kiang, Tibetan sandgrouse and black-necked cranes. In Arunachal Pradesh, India's easternmost state, he has witnessed exhausted migrant geese drop to the tarmac road at Sela Pass, at almost 14,000 feet, to drink from puddles. And in the wetlands of Assam and West Bengal he counts bar-headed geese at their winter grounds on reservoirs and lakes.

Sujan and I have many times watched flocks of bar-headed and eastern greylag geese together, as they fed in the grassy beels of Kaziranga, with lumbering one-horned rhinoceroses always somewhere near. We've seen lissom families of smooth-coated otters scamper past the geese, and hog deer and wild water buffalo grazing with them. In the park, where humans pose no threat, the geese graze through the day; but in central West Bengal, where a large dam harbours winter

The Meaning of Geese

flocks, they roost by day and move to fields to feed in the safety of darkness.

We talked of the rare geese – bean, whitefront, lesser whitefront – that Sujan has seen around his peerless country. 'A few years ago, a red-breasted goose was seen in Delhi,' he said. Astounded, I looked the record up. The bird was photographed with bar-headed geese at Bijnor in March 2014. The two birders who saw it had no idea what it was. As they were on the way to their village for Holi celebrations, it was several days before they asked a friend for identification help. This exquisite goose, lost, almost 2,000 miles from its species' nearest wintering grounds in Azerbaijan, was never seen again.*

As we said goodbye I wished Sujan and his family well, and wished him plenty of work once the Covid pandemic had passed. 'I'm fine,' he laughed. 'I just bought *All the Birds of the World*: 10,000 birds I can see without going anywhere! But you,' he barked, wrinkling his broad face in admonishment. 'You need to get your hair done. You can't go out looking like a porcupine.'

Friday 20th November

A week ago, Andy saw twenty-six Russian white-fronted geese on the grazing marsh at Holkham. Though a handful of whitefronts turn up every winter in our great flocks of pinkfeet, and already I have seen several across North Norfolk,

---

* A further red-breasted goose, a youngster, was photographed with eastern greylag geese at Nalsarovar in Gujarat in January 2021, during the writing of this book.

November

Holkham has been midwinter home to a discrete flock of these handsome birds for as long as records have been kept.

In the hope of seeing Andy's whitefronts, I set off on my bike today, once last night's frost had lifted. But I never made it to Holkham. North of the Barshams, passing a plantation wood, I spotted a freshly harvested field of maize through its open five-bar gate. I squeezed my brakes and spun my bike around, into the muddy gateway. Here, even with the naked eye, I could see a distant flock of birds. Just as my binoculars fell on the warm brown necks and blue-grey backs of pinkfeet, my ears caught the hard calls of greylags too. I leaned my bike against the gate, squelched through the deep mud to the edge of the wood, and out of the wind, set up my scope and entered the lives of geese.

In the late 1950s and early 1960s artist Charles Tunnicliffe illustrated four Ladybird books, depicting the seasons in the British countryside. Each charming watercolour plate portrays a habitat or country scene packed with the plants, birds, mammals and insects which a reader might then have expected to see in them. For as long as I watched today, I felt plunged into a Tunnicliffe plate from *What to Look for in Winter*.

Around 500 pinkfeet were at the rear edge of the field when I arrived, and with them more than 100 greylags. The geese were feeding, following harvested rows of maize, picking at fallen seed. From time to time a goose would find a whole cob, its dry grains the colour of my grandmother's butter. Raised on her father's North Norfolk farm, on milk from their herd of red poll cattle, until the day my grandmother died she never put her butter in a fridge, but kept it on a dish in the pantry, where its skin would turn a waxy gold. Finding a butter-golden cob, a lucky goose would grasp it by the husk and run, head back, breast forward, receiving jealous pecks from all the geese around it as it went.

The day's cloud broke; a blessed hour of winter sun began, lighting the greylags' orange bills and pale, stout necks. More even than the geese, the landscape and its many other birds seemed rendered in the loving paints of Tunnicliffe. The wood's edge, on my left, was noisy with house sparrows, blue tits and chaffinches, all of which from time to time would cast themselves into the stubble to feed. Across the front flank of the goose flock woodpigeons were gathered. Many sneer at woodpigeons; but those who sneer have surely never looked. The pure grey of a woodpigeon's head fades into a wine-stained breast. Silken patches of sea green, furrowed like a goose's neck, make a half collar, perched above a second collar formed of two unmelted spots of snow. A straw-yellow bill darkens – towards the pigeon's apple-juice eyes – to a red the colour of a scab on a ruffian's knee. A woodpigeon is magnificent.

Hundreds of woodpigeons wove across the field. Among them, here and there, I could see the grape-bloom blue of stock doves. Further back, around the geese, were jackdaws, high-stepping officiously across the warm brown earth. There were common gulls too, kind-faced but keen-eyed, strutting on putty-green legs. A wren gave his furious whirr from the hedge, a robin his watery trickle and, as if to add a focal drama to our artist's winter scene, two pheasant cocks marched across the field to meet each other, puffing burnished breasts in pride, trailing improbable tails.

All the time small groups of pinkfeet came and went, until the flock had built to around 800 birds. More greylags dropped in too, and in the field beyond far more were resting on a reservoir. Clouds gathered, the wind grew colder, strewing the tan November leaves of oaks across the earth, and I began to shiver. I left the geese, and all these many birds, thankful for having seen their winter pageant, and I cycled home.

Tuesday 24th November

Two weeks ago, James saw a black brant out by the East Hills in Wells Harbour. 'A typically smart adult bird,' he told me, which would 'no doubt soon be joining the flock at Wells.' Over the weekend it was seen again, both by the East Hills and at North Point, just to the east of the town. I thought this morning that I would try my luck.

It was milder by far than yesterday as I cycled north, so I quickly stuffed my gloves and buff into the pocket of my fleece and pushed my sleeves back to my elbows. There were still geese in Friday's maize field, but fewer, and my heart was set on saltmarsh brents. Despite the noisy skeins of pinkfeet strewing the sky above the long stretch north of Egmere, I pedalled on, through the flint-walled town of Wells and east to the North Point track.

Along the far shore of North Point pools hundreds of greylags were assembled, while on the landward side were pinkfeet. West of the track were two small groups of brents. I set my scope on them. Could finding the black brant really be so easy?

The birds were all our lovely dark-bellied brents, many of them youngsters, hatched in western Siberia just this year. Around them dozens of wigeon fed, plucking with dawn-blue bills at shoots exposed where the marsh's water had retreated. Wigeon may be less evocative than our geese, but they are mighty travellers from Siberia too. The males, copper-red since they arrived in early autumn, are moulting into breeding plumage now, their breasts blushing the faded pink of old upholstery, their round heads lustrous as brand-new conkers.

East of the track, my scope passed quickly over hundreds of proud-necked greylags and hundreds more pinkfeet, dainty beside them. I fell to watching other birds; birds I've missed while I've spent so much time with geese over recent weeks; birds which together mean a Norfolk marsh in winter. Hundreds of teal busied themselves around the muddy islands. Some of the males were assuming breeding plumage too, heads emerald and chestnut in the morning sun. Lapwings, round-bellied and satin-backed, turned black masks and crests into the southwest wind. Around their feet a dozen dunlin ran, fidgeting in search of winter food. And shelduck slept, immaculate in spite of lives defined by mud.

As I peered through my telescope, warm with the memory of hundreds of winter days spent watching these same birds with friends, I felt the joyous, juddering talk of brent geese in my chest. Dwellers of half-sea habitats, brents must visit freshwater every day to drink and to rinse salt from their feathers. It was my luck to be standing at North Point just as 300 of these beloved birds arrived, twisting madly as they came to land.

They spared no time in drinking, each goose dipping its stout black bill into the pool. Some began to bathe, splashing their breasts and necks repeatedly against the water, beating the surface with their wings, washing away the North Sea's cloying brine. Next they took to whiffling in the water, wildly turning upside down in it. Their baths accomplished, they beat their wings, drying them in readiness to fly.

November

As the birds bathed, I checked the flock from right to left, counting them and looking for any that were different. Ten geese from the left end of the flock I found the brant, a flawless adult as James had said. With a black brant's classic collar – joined in a wide white fan beneath the chin – the goose's back and belly were the colour of Green and Black's organic 85 per cent. Its flank patch was textbook too: wide, white and barely barred. As if in emphasis of its difference, the brant took to the wing alone, flying strongly north into the saltmarsh.

Little by little, in groups of fifty or so, the dark-bellied brent geese followed it. Their visit had taken only twenty minutes. By pure luck I had witnessed it and seen among them their lost Pacific companion. Among them, but genetically a continent apart.

Wednesday 25th November

In November 1926 Norfolk Naturalists Trust (known since 1994 as Norfolk Wildlife Trust) came into being. First of the county wildlife trusts, it was formed to own and care for Cley Marshes, which a group of twelve friends, led by Dr Sydney Long, had purchased in March of the same year for its ornithological importance. Reporting the trust's foundation in the *Eastern Daily Press*, Sydney Long wrote prophetically: 'one is anxious to preserve for future generations areas of marsh, heath, woods and undrained fenland (of which there still remain a few acres in the county) with their natural wealth of flora and fauna.'

The scope of Norfolk Wildlife Trust has grown enormously over almost 100 years and now embraces priceless reserves across the county; but Cley remains the crucible of the modern wildlife trusts and one of the homes of birdwatching. For decades birders have moved to Cley, drawn both by its avocets, bitterns, marsh harriers and bearded tits, and by the almost unequalled list of rare birds which have been recorded here and on neighbouring Blakeney Point.

I had to visit Cley by car today, so I arranged to meet my thoughtful friend Mark Golley. I hoped to see the landscape through his wild eyes, and perhaps to see the two pale-bellied brent geese he has been watching in the Eye Field. Mark came to Cley in 1990 as assistant warden to Bernard Bishop, whose father Billy had been warden for forty years and whose great-grandfather Bob was Cley's first watcher, appointed in 1926 by Sydney Long himself. Mark was seasonal warden until 1993 but has stayed in Cley, and ever since has watched and deeply loved the marsh's birds.

An otter has many times been seen in the Cley New Drain of late. With bearded tits chiming in the wintry reed and little grebes, puffed like soufflés, diving in the drain, I stood at the spot with Mark today, until a loud splash betrayed the otter's presence. Reed quivered at its base and a sharp tail waved in the glass-green water. Neither of us spoke; we barely breathed. We both grew up – Mark in Tarka country in the Southwest – in a time when to see an English otter was a fantasy. Even five years ago seeing an otter in Norfolk was rare. None of the thrill has faded, nor ever will.

Our otter – young and slender – fished along the reed's edge, crunching noisily each time it surfaced. The little grebes kept a wary eye, stretching their necks and gathering their fluffy skirts with all the prim disapproval of Edwardian ladies told a smutty joke. A kingfisher whistled by, its copper sulphate back at odds with the reeds' dun and the sea's grey and the winter white of the great North Norfolk sky.

We stood and waited, happy that such an animal has come back into our Norfolk rivers and our lives, but we saw no more. That is an otter's magic. Talking of speciation, species limits and of hybrids, we carried on. For several years Mark has known a mixed family of brent geese here, the gander a dark-bellied brent from Siberia, the goose a pale-belly perhaps from Svalbard, their offspring in between. The birds have yet to arrive this winter, though last winter they made their appearance as late as February.

In the Eye Field, the cheery trills of snow buntings all around, Mark spotted the brighter of this winter's two pale-bellied brents among the regular flock of dark-bellies. 'The nicest one I've seen here in many years,' he said, extolling its chalk-white flanks and belly.

'They look so gentle beside dark-bellied,' he added, lovingly. More brents flew in from Blakeney Harbour and this winter's second pale-belly appeared, at the back of the flock. This bird was dingier in the belly, smudged with a dusty grey. For Mark, these brent goose forms are valid species, breeding in distinct regions of the Arctic, wintering in separate temperate areas, and readily identifiable in the field. 'They're just so different,' he said excitedly, as we watched the smarter of the pale-bellied birds, the sci-fi calls of hundreds of golden plovers in our ears.

We walked on, south along the West Bank, discussing the taxonomy and identification of tundra and taiga bean geese, of Siberian and Stejneger's stonechats. I delighted in Mark's sharp mind and joyous love of birds, while little egrets fed beside us in a craze of saltmarsh pools and channels. Looking east, onto the reserve, Mark pointed to the spot where almost

The Meaning of Geese

forty years ago he saw his first black brant, where I remember great flocks of brents each winter of my schooldays. Each in the silence of his own mind we were thankful: for birds, for otters, for Sydney Long, for Norfolk Wildlife Trust, and, woven through all our lives along the Norfolk coast, the binding thread of geese.

DECEMBER

a heaving mass of blue-grey backs

As pinkfoot flocks reach their peak, December is Norfolk's most thrilling month for geese. Among the pinkfeet, I see a Todd's Canada goose, redolent with meaning, and two snow geese, of mysterious origins.

Tuesday 1st December

I was right when I mused in late September that a Todd's Canada goose would soon be borne from Lancashire to Norfolk in a flock of pinkfeet. Early in November Nick P. and Ash found one at Inmere in West Norfolk. They let me know straight away, but it was too late in the day for me to cycle so far. A few days later Ash and James saw it again, with a large pinkfoot flock, still further away at Snettisham. 'Don't worry,' Ash said, 'It'll be here for months. You'll see it when it comes closer.'

For the past two days it has poured, so I've read by my fire and written my thoughts on geese; but yesterday afternoon, in the rain, Nick found the Todd's again, much closer to home, to the south of Docking, in a vast flock of pinkfeet feeding on still unharvested beet. With them, strangely, there was also a pair of snow geese, looking for all the world like wild Nearctic wanderers, except for a ring on the leg of each bird: one a slim metal ring and the other in yellow plastic, both likely to be from captive collections.*

I got up at six today, to make the most of the promise of better weather. It was pouring still, but by dawn the rain was starting to pass. I switched on the flashing lights on my bike and pedalled towards the full moon. At the turning to Creake I made a mistake: I decided to take the Burma Road, the main road to King's Lynn, to save a lengthy detour through South Creake and Syderstone. This set me straight into a fickle wind; and each lorry tearing by in the early light whipped eddies fit to tip me over, to join the crumpled company of muntjac, pheasants, hares and roe whose rain-soaked corpses lined the roadside. I was glad to reach the turning north to Docking.

Leaving the pine-dark tunnel of Syderstone woods, I began to see and hear geese, hundreds and hundreds of birds, moving in jagged lines across the fretful sky towards Docking. As they neared the field, still far ahead of me, they broke from their ordered skeins: each goose, wings arched, locked on its own straight path to the ground and the beet.

---

* As winter progressed the story of these Norfolk snow geese became a little clearer. They were first seen roosting on Deepdale Marsh on 24th November, having been seen in Scotland in the morning on the same day. Much later, in July 2021, having been seen at numerous other sites, the geese were trapped by ringers on North Ronaldsay, Orkney, and it was found that the metal ring originated from the German bird zoo known as Weltvogelpark Walsrode.

December

My first sight of the field was of a heaving mass of blue-grey backs, more densely packed by far than any flock I've seen this winter; but as I stopped at the gate, before I had even dismounted my bike, something disturbed the far flank of the geese. Panic rippled through the flock towards me and wave after wave of birds took to the air. I was hit by the awesome thrum of their wings, filling my chest with sound. Then all these thousands of geese began to call, shrill headnotes above a deeper throbbing bark.

In spite of the many trucks and cars thundering by on the road, and in spite of the panic clearly having spread from the back edge of the flock, hundreds of metres away, I was worried my puny red bike and I had caused the birds to flee. I need not have been concerned. I stood for five hours quietly by the hedge, and in this time the mass of geese took to the air some five times more, always on hearing gunshot from the wood beyond, or flushed by a farmer's vehicle coming close. Each time the pinkfeet sprang into flight I felt the pulse of their wings; then every time they split into groups, with many thousands landing on a ridge of cereal stubble to my left. I had just found a barnacle goose among them here, half an hour after I arrived, when Nick P appeared in his van.

Nick had not been watching with me long when pinks began to peel from the hill and return to the sugar beet field. When geese come to land they almost hover for a moment, making a handful of angel-flaps, guiding themselves to the ground. This gives a wonderful chance to see them well, and to find the scarcer geese among them. My focus was locked on landing geese when I heard Nick's Yorkshire voice beside me. 'There are the snow geese,' he said, and I looked up. Cutting through thousands of fawn-chested pinks swirling above the ridge, two white geese shone in the day's dim light. They were with us throughout the day, these snows, always together, always feeding in the same distant reach of the field; one bird larger, and bigger billed, clearly the gander of the pair.

We pondered their origins. Snow geese are uncommon in captivity in the UK now and only rarely manage to escape. Wherever they're from, it's likely these are the same two birds which have toured the country through 2020. I'm intrigued – but untroubled – by the origin of these geese. I watch birds not to add them to a list of species seen; nor to sneer at birds which are not truly wild. I watch them because they are magnificent, as these snow geese looked today among many thousands of pinks.

The snow geese were not the only strangers in the flock. Each time the horde of birds came down to feed or flew to rest on the ridge, we scanned until our eyes wept in the wind. We found five barnacle geese in all. Nick saw a tundra bean goose too, but the flock was so vast and so dense that he lost it straight away and we never saw it again.

We were sure, after four hours grilling the birds, that the Todd's Canada goose was not among them. We were wrong. The last time we saw the geese fly up from the field to the ridge, Nick went back to his van to warm up with a mug of tea. Just then my scope fell on a sleeping bird with a black neck and a white strap through its cheek. I thought at first, at such great distance, among such a mêlée of birds, that I might be seeing a barnacle goose behind the body of a sleeping pinkfoot. Then another hundred pinkfeet came to land and the goose raised its slender neck.

In 2016, when I bought his lovely painting of a red-breasted goose and a Todd's Canada feeding among pinkfeet,

December

James told me he had hardly ever in all his years seen a feral Canada goose in our pinkfoot flocks. Though very rare, Todd's, which breeds as close to us as Greenland, is among the regional forms of wild Canada geese most frequently seen in the UK, arriving either with Greenland-breeding barnacle geese on Islay or with pinkfeet in eastern Scotland, Lancashire or Norfolk.

At first glance a Todd's, like the lovely bird we saw today, is similar to the feral Canada geese we casually dismiss as alien thugs. It is a large goose, its body clearly bigger than a pinkfoot's. Its mantle though is subtly darker than a feral bird's, with narrower pale fringes to each feather. Where a feral goose has a meal-white breast, Todd's Canada is honey-stained, palest close to the base of the neck. Its white cheek is narrow and squared at the top and – most distinctive of all – the goose's neck is short and slim in relation to its body, with the feeble look of a coat hanger hook. A size five goose with a size four neck.

After four weeks knowing this striking bird was here, always beyond the range of my legs and bike, I was thrilled to see it now. It was not just a wayward goose, but a link to my lost friend Sarah, who went with me to buy the painting now above my stairs, a year before she died. In a cold and muddy field today, I whispered to her I had seen a Todd's, my first since the bird in a painting which she loved.

Wednesday 2nd December

This has become another in a series of difficult winters for Norfolk's pinkfeet. As David Lyles told me in October, under pressure to drill wheat quickly, farmers now cultivate sugar beet fields as soon as they are harvested, and scare

The Meaning of Geese

geese off with gas guns, shotguns and trucks. Our hungry pinks have switched to foraging in harvested maize, now widely grown for anaerobic digesters, but here the pattern of early drilling with wheat and driving geese away is repeated. Lately small flocks of pinkfeet have been reported all over Norfolk, and further afield, in places where they have not been seen in living memory. Wise goose-watchers like Andy and James, who have studied the geese for decades, are worried their numbers are falling, that we might even lose our great pinkfoot flocks if they're left with nothing to eat; as we lost them once before, to disturbance following the Second World War.

The vast flock which Nick and I watched near Docking yesterday has been feeding on unharvested beet for at least ten days. The birds have stripped the leaves from the furthest third of the field and have scalped the roots, exposing nutritious white flesh. Neither Nick nor I could understand why the farmer had left them to feed for so long when, unlike in harvested beet, they were eating his profit from the crop. Early this morning, before I went out on my bike, I wrote to David, asking what he thought.

It was clear and cold overnight, and I left home under bullfinch-bellied clouds. The moon was still fat, but one edge had now gone, like a rind cut away from a cheese. Along lanes between Creake and Syderstone hundreds of blackbirds fed on haws and a party of fieldfares burst from a holly at my approach, dropping their harsh, percussive calls.

At Barwick I heard a mistle thrush, my first in song since spring, but the sky's few pinkfeet were all heading south, away from yesterday's beet. Not a single goose was in the field when I arrived, though many were still on the stubble ridge behind. Clanging machines, across the road, were lifting a field of carrots, spitting out plumes of sandy soil, filling the air with a sickly smell.

Nick and Ash arrived as I set up my scope. They had been past this morning already and had seen that something was keeping the geese from coming to feed; most likely the carrot harvest. Soon after they started watching with me, the birds sprang as one from the stubble and circled the field. 'Five thousand,' said Ash, 'or in that range.' The flock was a third as large – a quarter perhaps – as at yesterday's deafening peak. We could see that they wanted to land and feed, with small groups splintering from the mass, wheeling above the beet, but none would come down. Many returned to the ridge to wait; others flew off to the north and were gone. 'It's not gonna happen,' Ash said. 'You want them to fit in a pattern, but it's different each time. Just a few birds land, and it's like a switch. They won't today.'

So Nick and Ash drove on, to search for geese around Bircham and Fring. I stayed by the field, alone, but for a blue tit skipping along the winter-barren hedge, and the last mauve blooms of fodder radish by my feet, in defiance of last night's frost.

Until this Covid year, most humans in the Global North had lost an ancestral knowledge of death. Most of us are never cold, homeless or hungry. Most infectious diseases have been emasculated, by vaccines, antibiotics and intensive care. And, unlike hundreds of millions of people across the tropics, we no longer live with animals likely to kill us. The geese, though, live with the knowledge of death. Theirs is a daily calorific grind; and disturbance at feeding fields can cost them dear. Theirs is a world in which red fox, Arctic fox, gyrfalcon, great skua, exhaustion and the gun are present dangers. While we enjoy the warmth and

The Meaning of Geese

comfort of our homes, the geese are exposed to every mood of nature. A full moon lets them forage in the greater safety of the night, and rest by day, but if, as lately, cloud and rain obscure the moon, the geese can get lost or lose a whole night's feeding. Wind, fog, snow, frost, tide, moon and humans: we all affect the fortunes of our cackling brethren of the north.

I was lost in the knife-edge lives of geese, when two tractors and a harvester lumbered onto the field, where yesterday at least 15,000 pinks had fed. I made to go home, dismantling my scope, but my phone whirred with a text from Ash: they had found a feeding flock in harvested beet, on Pound Lane, east of Docking. I cycled two miles further to meet them there. The birds were calm, letting me pedal past, to where Nick and Ash were sheltering from the bitter drizzle in their van. A barnacle goose was at the front edge of a flock of several thousand pinks, chattering as they picked at sugar beet tops. Leaning against the van, in the murk, I struggled to see through my rain-spattered scope, but Ash found two tundra bean geese, one of them huge, with a notch of white at the base of its bill. 'That's a leggy bird,' I said. 'They always look long-legged to me,' Ash replied. 'I love the way they move across the ground, as though they're limping.'

As the drizzle worsened, and clouds came down to snuff the light, I chose to head for home. Cycling through fifteen miles of raw and unrelenting rain, I let myself, for one vain moment, imagine a kinship between the geese and me: Arctic birds and a wheezing cyclist, together against the elements of winter. But of course my bike and I mean nothing to them.

My phone rang when I got home. It was David, with news of beet and birds. The farmer at Docking was his friend, who had chosen to let the birds feed, provided the harm they did to his crop was not too great. 'They've started harvesting there today,' he said. 'They'll be done tonight. It's worth going back as the geese will be feeding tomorrow on the tops.' We talked of his worry that, starved of beet, the birds could move into fields of oilseed rape. 'They live such long lives,' David said. 'It takes them time to learn a behaviour, and when they do they stick with it. The last thing we need is for them to move into oilseed rape. The conflict would be so much worse.'

I thanked David for sharing his farming insight again. 'I don't have much,' he laughed in reply. 'I've just been around a long time.'

Thursday 3rd December

Tuesday's snow geese reappeared today, in less evocative surroundings, with a group of greylags in the Wensum Valley. Their choice of company has not enhanced their credentials as true wild birds. There is, however, one wild snow goose in the UK this winter, a fabulous blue goose in a Scottish flock of pinkfeet. A returning bird, first found in 2017, it has lately been seen at several sites across the Highlands, including today at Nigg.

Two subspecies of snow geese are recognised. The greater snow goose breeds in northeast Canada and northwest Greenland, wintering on the east coast of the USA. The lesser snow goose is far more populous and widespread, breeding through Arctic Canada, in Alaska and as far as northeast Siberia. It winters right across the southern states, in northern Mexico and in Japan. The majority of snow geese are pure white, with black primary feathers and a snarling carmine bill, but a significant percentage of lesser snows are a lustrous purplish black, with a blue-grey mantle and a pure white face, framed by a stout black neck. These are blue geese. The two colour forms breed together and between them there exists a range of intergrades. Some, like the gander seen today in Scotland, are dark but have a white head and upper neck, and a frosty rump and belly.

My friend Tim Stowe has family in Inverness and often travels north to see his grandsons. Twice this autumn he has seen this magnificent goose among the pinkfeet there. I have longed for it to be carried south to Norfolk with the pinks but, since it has wintered in the Highlands for four years now, there is little hope it will.

Oddly though, the first blue snow goose seen in Europe may well have been here in Norfolk. In *The Eye of the Wind* Peter Scott quotes an entry in his shooting diary, from Terrington in West Norfolk on the 13th December 1929. He describes a goose he felt at the time was a partial albino greylag but later, having travelled in North America, he came to realise was a blue goose.

Peter Scott will forever be more nearly associated with a white snow goose. Before the Second World War he lived in the East Lighthouse near Sutton Bridge, where the River Nene flows into the Wash on Norfolk's farthest edge. Here he painted, and gathered around him a collection of waterfowl, both captive-bred and birds which he had injured shooting and later tamed. In *The Snow Goose*, a hauntingly lovely story which Paul Gallico first published in 1940, the lonely artist Rhayader who lives in a lighthouse and creates a sanctuary for waterfowl, is immediately recognisable as Peter Scott.

December

A friend of Scott's suggested taking legal action for the slight, but a happier settlement was reached when the artist was asked to illustrate the British edition. There is nothing in the book, in fact, save for the character's physical deformity, which could be construed as damaging to Scott. Rather it is a eulogy to Rhayader's nobility of character. The fictional artist deeply loves the wild birds which yearly come back from the Arctic to his protected marsh, to join the captive birds which live there with him.

One autumn day a girl from the village, Frith, appears at Rhayader's door, her fear of the reclusive hunchback overcome by concern for the wounded bird in her arms. It is a snow goose, a young bird of the year which has been shot, having reached the UK in a savage storm. Together they heal the goose, which takes to following Rhayader, but in the spring it breaks his heart by flying north with the many wild pinkfeet which have wintered with him.

In autumn, miraculously, the goose returns and this becomes the pattern of several years, until one spring the snow goose stays, as though paired with Rhayader himself. In late May of that year, Rhayader hears the call and takes his boat across the channel to Dunkirk, leaving his birds in the care of Frith who by now is a beautiful young woman. The snow goose follows him.

Rhayader is observed heroically rescuing British troops, returning tirelessly to the beach, the snow goose always flying above his boat; until he himself is lost. Finally, in a passage impossible to read without tears, the snow goose comes back alone, bringing the knowledge that Frith held already in her heart, that the man she loved has died.

'And so, when one sunset she heard the high-pitched, well-remembered note cried from the heavens, it brought no instant of false hope to her heart.'

The Meaning of Geese

Friday 4th December

I rarely remember dreams, but I woke up deep in the night, aware I had dreamed of geese. Early this morning as I lay in bed, listening to Radio Four, I gazed at the heartless snow-grey sky and, in the distance, fifteen hundred pinkfeet headed west. December, as our flocks of pinkfeet swell to their peak and spread out across the county, is – more than any other – Norfolk's month of geese.

Saturday 5th December

When my parents first married they briefly left Norfolk while my doctor father worked at a hospital in Cheltenham. From here they visited Slimbridge, headquarters of the Wildfowl and Wetlands Trust, where they bought a copy of Peter Scott's *A Coloured Key to the Wildfowl of the World.* My mother had loved ducks since her earliest childhood when, on the day of my aunt's christening, she was given a newly hatched Aylesbury duckling to raise. As a young birder I adored this book, endlessly studying its charming plates until I had memorised all of the swans, geese and ducks in the world. On the page dedicated to *Branta* geese Peter Scott illustrates four forms of the brent goose: dark-bellied, pale-bellied (which he calls light-bellied), black brant and the enigmatic Lawrence's brent goose, which we know today as the grey-bellied brant.

Scott's text account for the grey-bellied brant describes a bird whose breeding area was still unknown, and which he thought might never have existed as a distinct population. The grey-bellied brant is still not recognised by any taxonomic authority, but we now know greatly more about this distinctive bird, including that it breeds on Melville, Eglington and Prince Patrick Islands in the Canadian Arctic. In the UK our understanding of vagrant grey-bellied brants has been revolutionised by the publication, in autumn 2020, of a paper in the journal *British Birds* by Norfolk's James McCallum.

From early 2017 until the start of 2020, a single gander of this cryptic bird visited Norfolk every winter with pink-footed geese. It was first filmed as a juvenile, in January 2017, in a large flock of pinks near Docking. The observers did not know what they had seen until late the same year, when James found the returning goose as an adult and mooted its identity. Since then, he has observed it more often and more carefully than anyone else. This goose, its remote Arctic home, and its subtle plumage, have dwelt on James's mind and inspired his creativity. His exhaustive paper describes and illustrates – in words, photographs and paintings – the identification of the Norfolk grey-bellied brant, relative to the three other geographic forms of the brent goose, and to hybrids between them. It is remarkable.

On Saturday last week, in the great flock at Docking, Nick observed a perplexing young brent goose. For a brent to be alone with pinks is unusual enough, but this bird, seen fleetingly among thousands of much larger pinkfeet, seemed to show characteristics of a grey-bellied brant. On Tuesday, when he and I were watching the flock together, Nick said, 'Oh there's the brent.' I assumed he meant a lost dark-bellied brent which several of us have now seen with the pinks. But no, he explained, this was a different bird, a youngster, half-seen on Saturday. Following his directions, I found it in a scrum of pinks, but neither of us could see any more than its neck. At such a distance, under drizzle,

The Meaning of Geese

the necks of all forms of juvenile brent geese are as good as identical.

An hour later we found the bird again, right at the back of the field, dwarfed once again by busily feeding pinks. We would see its head for a moment, then a flash of its flank, but could never see the whole bird, nor – crucially – judge the colour of its body, nor the pattern of its belly and vent.

Just once we saw the whole bird in the open, during a blessed break in the clouds, which let the lovely amber light of winter warm the field. Though it was far to the back of the flock, we both were struck by the goose's dark belly, contrasting with a bold white flank, and by the brown tones of its mantle. 'The colour of wet clay earth,' I said to Nick.

Yesterday, in driving rain and sleet, Nick and Ash spent hours in their van, watching the same huge flock of pinkfeet feeding on leftover beet. They saw the Todd's and several Russian whitefronts, and Ash took a film of the distant brent. He sent it at once to James, who shelved his tax return and hurried to Docking, only to find the throng of geese lost in a flurry of snow.

This morning I cycled to Docking and the field of harvested beet, hoping to see this confusing brent again. I had not been there for long, when James appeared, as I knew he would. First among Norfolk's goose-watchers, his eye for detail is astonishing. He needed to see the goose for himself and tease out what it was.

'Morning young man,' he said as he arrived; to which I joked that, having cycled 499 miles this autumn, I was feeling anything but young. The field had largely been stripped of tops, most likely overnight, and the geese were resting on their favoured stubble ridge. James quickly found the Todd's Canada goose among them, its colours

December

caramelised in the kind light following last night's frost; but the geese were jumpy. Thousands took flight as a Chinese water deer cantered through them and many more were put up by a pheasant shoot nearby. Little by little the geese moved on, to an unharvested field on the Burnham Market road which James had found this morning. We agreed to meet again there.

The field was only a mile to the north, taking me to 500 miles cycled after geese this autumn: a risible milestone beside the journeys undertaken by our geese. From the edge of Docking, we crept along a hedge and crouched among alexanders shoots to survey the mounting flock of geese. James handed me a thick spongy mat to sit on. 'Essential kit for painting,' he said. 'I don't know what it is but I think it comes from the offshore wind farms. I find it washed up on the beach. I've got two rolls in the garage at home.'

'The geese in the field will draw them in from all around now,' James said, as the first skein came to join the feeding birds. 'I don't understand it. In all my years I've never seen a farmer leave the geese to feed on unharvested beet. Most would be driving them off every hour.'

A barnacle goose was on the edge of the flock, and in the middle a handsome family of tundra beans, goose, gander and one youngster. They remained alert the whole time that we watched, the adults' thick necks ramrod straight. 'They look as though they're newly in,' James said. 'Maybe they're wondering what's going on: we weren't allowed to feed in unharvested beet in the Netherlands.'

In autumn and winter, when geese fill Norfolk's marshes, fields and skies, James feels most alive. Hunkered with him in the hedge, I confessed I struggled with winter's cold and darkness, and that spring's first chiffchaff flooded me each year with hope. 'What's wrong with you man?' He scolded, laughing. 'I love the dynamic movement of autumn, and the geese in winter. When spring comes I'm always thinking: oh no, already? I want another month. I'm just not ready for the quickening of pace.'

Our talk inevitably shifted to grey-bellied brants and the chance that the juvenile bird we sought was Norfolk's second. 'Bloomers and I had thought about them for years,' he said, referring to Andy Bloomfield, 'wondering if one would ever come to Norfolk. We always thought it would be with pinkfeet. I was planning to go to Ireland, to have a look at the ones which turn up there, but then ours arrived.'

I praised his outstanding paper. 'Nobody seemed interested. It's just an intergrade, they said, and you'll never prove it is one anyway. The more people doubted it, the harder I worked to find out about them in their home range. It's been one of the most satisfying birds for me.' He warmed, describing the brant's unique colour. 'The back feathers are almost like a barnacle's, only brown. When you really look you see there's a dark subterminal bar and then a pale fringe. There's a similar pattern on pale-bellies, but you just don't see it on dark-bellies or black brants or their hybrids.'

Here was a master, whose thousands of hours, over thirty years, spent in the company of geese, had bestowed on him a unique stake in their world, and a rare ability to share their lives with his paints. Our conversation roamed across the globe, taking in taiga bean geese in the Yare, cackling geese whose nests he'd found in Alaskan tundra, and the eastern greylags and bar-headed geese which it has been my privilege to watch innumerable times in India.

Mostly we spoke of our native Norfolk and her geese. When we touched on greylags and their spread, I mentioned the release of eight birds at Ranworth in 1933. James, for whom nature writing often skims across the surface of a subject, cocked his head and flashed a smile.

'Maybe your book will be worth reading,' he said.

Thursday 10th December

Only two geese have a Holarctic distribution, breeding right around the northern tundras of Europe, Asia and North America. One is the brent goose, three of whose geographical forms – dark-bellied, pale-bellied and black brant – I have seen on my bike this year. James and I discussed the fourth – the grey-bellied brant – a few days ago, while we sheltered by a hedge.

The second Holarctic species is the greater white-fronted goose. Taxonomists disagree on the number of its regional forms, but (excluding the birds which have lately settled to breed in the Netherlands) all are long-distance migrants between Arctic breeding grounds and temperate winter grounds. Breeding in western Alaska and wintering along the Pacific coast of North America, from California south to Mexico, the Pacific white-fronted goose is the smallest of the American forms. In places it can be seen in winter beside the larger, darker tule white-fronted goose, which breeds only around Cook Inlet in Alaska, and winters in Central California, in the Sacramento and Suisun marshes. The most widespread of the American forms is Gambel's white-fronted goose, which breeds across the north of Alaska and Canada and winters largely in coastal states around the Gulf of Mexico. It is known to US wildfowlers as the specklebelly, on account of the black blotches shown by all adult greater whitefronts.

The Meaning of Geese

Two forms of the same species winter in the British Isles. The striking Greenland white-fronted goose breeds in western Greenland, migrates through Iceland and winters in Scotland, the Hebrides and Ireland, plus in small numbers in North West England and North Wales. The Russian white-fronted goose breeds right across Arctic Russia, from Europe to Chukotka. It winters in many temperate regions of Eurasia, including Northwest Europe, the steppes of Central Europe, the Black Sea, the marshes of Iraq, and wetlands in eastern China, the Korean Peninsula and Japan. This lovely bird is the whitefront familiar to English birders. It is the scarcest and last to arrive of the three geese whose flocks grace North Norfolk every winter.

Russian white-fronted geese have been known on Holkham's grazing marshes since records began. For Henry Stevenson, in the 1860s and 70s, the Russian whitefront was far less common than it is today: 'This goose is considered by Lord Leicester to be rare at Holkham, except in hard weather, when it commonly appears in flocks of from five to ten, and, being less shy, is easier of approach than others.' Andy now sees a flock of between 250 and 350 whitefronts every year. Still more use Holkham as a staging ground on spring migration, he believes, as the flock usually swells in late winter. His highest count at this time was of 800 birds.

As I cycled along the north edge of Holkham Park this morning, I caught sight of a small flock close to the road in morning sunshine. After several days of rain and fog, this sunshine alone was a treat. I pulled to the side of the road, assuming that the birds would all be greylags, but a sweep of my binoculars revealed both whitefronts and pinkfeet among them.

December

The only place to lean my bike was the sturdy, creosoted gatepost. With the geese so close to the road, I was worried that setting up my scope would spook them. The birds, though, showed no concern; today's whitefronts as confiding as their Victorian ancestors. With the huge pinkfoot flocks which roam North Norfolk, the best we can do is estimate how many birds are present, but here was a small flock in a single field, so I counted every one: two Egyptian geese alone by a flood, seventy-one greylags, five pinkfeet and thirty-one Russian whitefronts. The pinks were a pair with one youngster of this year, plus a single gander also with a young bird. Among the whitefronts there were just three young, two with one adult pair, and a singleton with another.

When James and I were watching geese last week, we joked that Norfolk's introduced, non-migratory greylags had grown fat in the county's marshes. We had both seen a small juvenile greylag with pinkfeet early in the season; a bird far slighter than our residents, and likely to have been a wanderer from Iceland. Likewise, beside our looming local greylags, today's Russian whitefronts looked wonderfully petite, their neat pink bills cropping the bright grass meant for Holkham's sheep and cattle.

Behind the geese, beneath the hedge, moorhens flicked out Morse code messages with their undertails, and sleepy teal were gathered by the ditch. Mallards blundered between the geese, each duck shadowed by a bottle-headed drake, his hormones keen for next spring's breeding. Skylarks purred above me, and a second pair of Egyptian geese flew in from the park, marching preposterously across the field, white shoulders flared, shattering the morning's idyll with their braying.

The whitefronts grazed, unmoved. As T. H. White observes in *The Book of Merlyn*, they are 'very beautiful creatures, the

The Meaning of Geese

wild White-Fronted Geese, whom, once a man has seen them, he will never forget.' White intended his book to be published during the Second World War, as the final part of the work which came to be known as *The Once and Future King*; but it was only in 1977, after his death, that *The Book of Merlyn* was released.

At the story's start, Merlyn appears before Arthur, on the eve of what the king knows must be his final battle. Arthur is heavy-hearted, reflecting on all that he has done, right and wrong, in his long life, and the many people he has lost. It is decades since last he saw his tutor and, at first, he imagines him a dream. Although his reign is done, Merlyn has come to teach Arthur some final lessons in kingship. He transports him to a badger's sett, where his erstwhile friends, a cast of animals, are gathered: hedgehog, badger, tawny owl, goat and grass snake, among others. Slowly – emotion welling within him – the king recalls his boyhood, spent among animals, learning open-heartedly from them.

Merlyn reveals that Arthur must visit the lives of two more animals, the second of them the white-fronted goose. Waking from his first night as a goose, taking off in a giant whirr of wings, among thousands of his kind, Arthur feels a forgotten joy. He falls into conversation with Lyó-lyok, a young female goose, who is soon disgusted by his questions on their nature and his comparisons with human warfare.

The geese, Arthur learns, have a high-minded, egalitarian society: frank and direct, but in all things honourable and fair. They pair for life; take turns to watch for danger as others graze; share resources, save for their nests which all geese know as sacrosanct; and appoint their leaders according to merit and experience.

Though T. H. White was a countryman, and a careful observer of wildlife, it would be naïve to read too much into the nobility of his geese. He was a complex man, troubled by nationalism and its role in the Second World War, and he makes no claim that his story – peopled, as it is, by magicians and talking animals – is more than allegory. But what his geese embody perfectly (prophetically, decades before the scale of our environmental harm became apparent) is our moral duty to take no more resources than are reasonable for our wellbeing, and to live equitably beside our fellow humans and the rest of biodiversity.

For it is with pity that White's white-fronted geese look on humankind: 'We have been on the earth for millions of years longer than you have, poor creatures, so you can hardly be blamed.'

Friday 11th December

I spoke today to Professor Jeff Price of the Tyndall Centre for Climate Change Research at the University of East Anglia, whom I know through our respective roles at Norfolk Wildlife Trust. A kind and quietly spoken soul, with wild hair and beard, and eyes which sparkle intelligently from behind his spectacles, Jeff is just the kind of scientist whose brilliant models are ignored by policymakers in disaster movies. With catastrophic consequences.

Jeff is an avid birder too, and a lover of geese, who spent last Sunday sifting through pinkfeet and whitefronts at the RSPB's Buckenham Marshes in the Broads. Professionally, among other projects, he coordinates the Wallace Initiative, a collaboration between scientists at UEA and James Cook University in Australia, which has modelled the effects of

The Meaning of Geese

various predicted climate change scenarios on 135,000 terrestrial species. The project is based on the timeless understanding, in Jeff's words to me today, that 'species tend to shift with climate. They always have.'

An extraordinary interactive map on the Wallace Initiative website illustrates predicted shifts in range for the many species which have been modelled. As we spoke today, Jeff tapped the names of geese into the search bar, to generate maps of their predicted responses to varying climate change scenarios. For pinkfeet, a rise in global temperature of just 1.5°C – unavoidable even assuming full compliance with the terms of the Paris Agreement – would shift their winter range far enough north to miss Norfolk almost completely. Thus, even should Norfolk farmers and conservationists offer perfect feeding for pinkfeet in harvested fields of beet and maize, Jeff's models predict we are doomed to lose this wondrous bird whose flocks epitomise our winter. 'With short-stopping,' Jeff told me, in his unswerving way, 'we lose species at the southern end of their ranges as it gets warmer. The balance of evidence is that many of the geese are shifting and they're soon not going to be here. They will simply stay further north.'

For whitefronts, the models predict that a 2°C rise in global average temperature – still likely even if the terms of the Paris Agreement are fully met – would render almost the whole of the species' breeding range in Asia unsuitable, plus much of the range in North America, including the entire breeding range of Pacific and tule white-fronted geese. For Arctic-breeding species there is no option to migrate further or move uphill. A catastrophic loss of breeding territory translates inexorably into a collapse of winter populations too.

December

Even where geographical space exists for species, including geese, to adjust their ranges in the face of human-induced climate change, other threats arise. 'The velocity of climate change is a concern. Can species continue to adapt?' Jeff is worried that birds forced by rising temperature to shift their ranges may struggle to feed. 'Are the new sites with appropriate climate providing the resources species need? What about their physiology in relation to climate? Birds need enough calories to get them through the night. The amount they need is related to overnight temperature.'

'Many species are shifting their migrations,' he continued. 'Some migrate earlier, some later. Changes in time can mean they miss their food sources.' Of equal concern is the likely reduction in the quality of food available, both to wild species and to humans. 'As atmospheric carbon dioxide goes up, there's a phenomenon called carbon fertilisation. You get more foliage but not necessarily more seed. In environmental chambers, under perfect conditions, you can get higher yields, but in the field you don't.'

'If you increase the ratio of carbon dioxide to nitrogen in the atmosphere, plants contain less protein, perhaps ten or fifteen per cent less protein. This has population-level effects. We are already seeing smaller cattle and smaller sheep. We don't yet know whether this is because it is hotter or because of reduced protein in their diets. Other micronutrients are known to change too, and this has been proven to affect humans. Perhaps it also affects geese.'

As temperature rises, die-offs, through infectious disease, are known to become more prevalent among wildfowl too. 'Where large flocks of waterfowl are crammed together, resting and feeding in the same places, under higher temperatures you can get mass mortality through botulism. This is well known in North America.'

Numbed by his words, I asked Jeff how – faced daily by the knowledge of our collapsing climate and biodiversity – he managed to stay focused on his work. 'My colleagues call me Dr Doom,' he answered, laughing ironically. 'None of these unknowns will make things better.' He paused a moment. 'We can do better. We all realise that what we do locally matters. With China decarbonising and the Biden election, things are changing. But, frankly, it makes me want to win the lottery and see all these things before they are extinct.'

Tuesday 15th December

I have never loved geese more than I do today. I am shivering by a field, my face licked by a winter wind. A mound of bramble stems ensnares my trouser legs and half my field of view is blacked out by the hawthorn hedge in which I'm hidden. Three red haws quiver in a cluster by my face – like triplets on a stave – and all around me there are geese.

The nearest pinks are only fifty metres from me. For two hours I have hidden in my hedge, letting this huge flock work towards me, over harvested beet. Thousands of geese are lost from view, feeding in the shallow dip which cuts across the muddy field. Thousands more are in the distance, where the undulating ground slopes up towards a hedge. Close by me hundreds feed; so close that I can hardly move.

I am by Crabbe Road, facing south. The sun, heavy in December's sky, is tracking west behind the flock. The geese are shining; their wings' pale tracery silvered by the low midwinter light. A gander stretches, raising a leg, reaching his left wing back. Lit from behind, his foot's pink webs are – for an instant – lipstick bright. His head tilts, his left eye glints. I love these moments with the lives of geese.

More pinks come from the north, from Holkham's coastal grass: loud groups of a dozen or a hundred; one holding more than fifteen hundred birds. As each skein comes, sinuous in Tuesday's cold blue sky, it strikes the light: the geese's shoulders glowing molten gold, their bellies bright. The very moment that a group begins descent, each goose breaks into calling, family members shrilly guiding one another to the ground.

I see why many of the geese have drifted quite so close to me. All through the past few days of unforgiving fog and rain, the birds have fed here. Up to 20,000 pinkfeet have been seen. By now, much of the bounty of the field has been consumed. The furthest birds are mostly sleeping. Those which are awake mill aimlessly, pecking at the ground from time to time. The closest geese, by contrast, forage fast, heads down, snatching hurriedly at shards of wasted beet. This is the richest place to feed, where most sweet beet remains, but it is also risky. These pinks are closest to the road; to the people, cars and tractors which have no doubt spooked them many times this week.

Just by the hedge a dunnock in a dirty puddle takes a bath, launching droplet constellations as it shakes. Beyond, I hear a wren's aggressive trill. I have been low of late, brooding, almost broken. Cycling in search of brents and pinkfeet sounds romantic, but in winter it is hard. After days of rain, and at the peak of sugar harvest, Norfolk's roads are wet and muddy. Every lorry chugging by, no matter how respectfully, spatters my clothes, my bike and shades with grime. The wind makes winter cycling all the harder, buffeting me off my course. Toughest of all – edging me into a wild creature's

The Meaning of Geese

world – is thermoregulation. Each time I cycle ten miles in a base layer, even on the coldest day, I'm quickly hot and sweaty. I find a flock of geese, and pull on fleeces, gloves and hat, but, after two hours standing hunkered by a hedge, inevitably I'm shaking.

In February my mother was diagnosed with a condition likely, one day, to be serious. In March she learned, in consequence, that she was vulnerable to Covid complications. She and my stepfather retreated into isolation, from which even now they've not emerged. Their dog – a gentle golden retriever, old before his time – has largely kept them happy; his warm face shoved into their laps, no matter how bleak the day.

Three weeks ago, quite suddenly, he died. It was a tiny tragedy – nothing in the context of this Covid year – but it was one which hurt the people I most love. I sped the following morning to their garden, where, awkward and distant, standing more than the requisite metres apart, we spoke, as we've spoken all this year. They sobbed and – powerless – I could neither hug nor comfort them.

They asked if I would stay with them for Christmas. So, more than a week ago, I did a fortnight's shopping, told friends and neighbours to stick away, and came into isolation. I have left home only twice, to cycle in search of geese. Mostly, it has rained, or it has been too foggy to cycle safely on our roads. I've stayed at home. Since March this year, I've been essentially alone, and without work. I've coped. I don't know why these past few days have felt so crushing. In part, I'm sure, it's the stark fear of taking Covid with me to my parents' home.

Now though, entangled in a hawthorn hedge, and shivering, I'm lost, like Arthur, in the bustle of a flock of geese. The nearest pinkfeet are so close to me, the low sun burnishing their breasts and necks. One family charges at another which has strayed too near, the goose and gander stretching out their necks in threat. Those chased, and chastened, jump away, necks back, chests forward, pink legs working double-time. Still more geese come, behind me, the cold day full of Arctic voices as they arch their wings and plane down to the mud.

I could not love them more.

Thursday 17th December

I needed brents today; needed their rugby-ball roundness and their throaty Russian voices. Three days ago, watching pinks on harvested beet, I saw small groups of dark-bellied brents fly over them, heading inland to feed on winter cereals. I therefore knew the geese had left our coastal saltmarsh and I would surely find some in the grazing marsh by Lady Anne's Drive.

Duly, I went there this morning, cycling on a bright, cold day past pigs, snout-deep in winter mud, past prick-eared tups and Holkham's barrel-bellied belted Galloways. The brents were where I knew they'd be, dozens dipping their conical bills to drink from one of the serpentine pools dug recently for wildlife on the National Nature Reserve. At the back of the grassy field there were dozens more, plenty of pin-striped youngsters with them.

As brent flocks always seem to be, the birds were busy; black heads tilted down, plucking at the sward with near-mechanical efficiency. There was tension in the flock – there always is – Siberian turf wars acted out on Norfolk's coastal grass. One gander pinned another to the ground – something I've never seen before – the loser freezing in submission on the grass. All the while the whole flock chattered, telling tales of tundra summers, of down-lined nests scattered like moons around a rough-legged buzzard eyrie, of June-brown Arctic foxes harried by the hawks, away from the downy chicks of buzzards and geese alike.

The brents were not alone. Pinkfeet were grazing here and there around them and, closely packed between two lines of brents, there was a flock of greylags. Even they, stout orange bills aglow, were not the largest geese here. With them there were several feral Canada geese, the first I've seen since September.

I will hear nothing said against feral Canada geese, though they are almost universally despised. They have a patrician elegance not shared by any other of our common geese. When most geese feed their necks bend, at the mid-point, almost at a right angle; the basal half held horizontal and the distal angled down. The slender, ink-black necks of feeding Canada geese, especially of the larger east-coast subspecies from which our introduced British birds derive, are so long they seem to hold an extra upward curve, between the two planes seen on other geese.

The birds today were larger than the vagrant Todd's Canada goose I twice saw around Docking recently: bigger-bodied, longer-necked. They were paler too, their chests oat-white in the morning's happy light. One Canada gander attacked a pair of greylags as I watched, curling his hydra neck and charging them into a ditch. Holkham's muscular greylags are unused to being weaker than the other geese they meet.

Canada geese, Janet Kear explains in *Man and Wildfowl*, were brought to England around 1665, for the waterfowl collection of King Charles II. By 1785, she says, they were breeding freely on country estates. The first national census of

December

Canada geese, in 1953, found between 2,600 and 3,600 birds. Already, by this time, they were unpopular with farmers.

In 1957 Peter Scott and Hugh Boyd – first staff biologist at what is now the Wildfowl and Wetlands Trust – published *Wildfowl of the British Isles*, in which feral Canada geese are described as very local in distribution, with much the largest population, around 1,000 birds, to be found at Holkham. Their solution to conflict between Canada geese and farmers is nothing short of astounding to modern conservationists. Over the previous four years, they explain, the Wildfowl Trust had caught moulting birds in problem areas and moved them to suitable localities across the country to found new colonies.

In this way the feral Canada goose was seeded across England, setting it up to colonise the whole country. The population rapidly increased, Kear writes, particularly along the Thames, in the West Midlands and in Yorkshire. Wildfowlers could do little to stem the species' spread, as the birds were generally too tame to hunt. By 1976 the UK supported almost 20,000 birds and by 1985 there were 39,000. As many of the geese were hand-tame residents of city parks, lethal control, Kear felt, would be unpopular. Today, the British Trust for Ornithology estimates a UK Canada goose population of 165,000 birds, including 55,000 pairs.

My whole Norfolk life I have lived with geese: brents, pinkfeet and whitefronts along the coast in winter, Canadas year-round on inland water, and lately greylags. The wild geese shape my winter, and the joyful whoops of Canadas announce my spring. For many in the UK, feral Canadas are the only geese they know, and love. Surely this makes them precious: friendly, snake-necked surrogates for a megafauna lost, white-cheeked splinters of a shattered wild.

The Meaning of Geese

Sunday 20th December

This winter four black brants have come to Norfolk, a number not matched in twenty years. A few days after I visited Cley, one joined the brent flock there. The brant I watched spurning the dark-bellies at North Point is still here too, and has been seen as far inland as Walsingham. In recent days, a textbook black brant has been much admired and photographed at Titchwell and at Choseley.

The fourth is a mysterious bird which, for a decade now, has intermittently been seen around the lovely village of Binham, where one line of my family has lived and farmed for generations. I went today, in hopes of seeing it.

The sun went with me, cutting three days' cloud like Philip Pullman's subtle knife, stealing me into another world. I cycled north along the Stiffkey valley, alders blushing in the morning light, and quick with siskins; squat oaks warmly ivy-wrapped.

As I found no geese at Binham, I cycled northwest, towards Stiffkey, then east to Cockthorpe, along two sides of an upturned triangle of roads through fields of wheat. To the east I noticed distant groups of geese in flight, blotches of birds, betraying themselves as brents. Brent flocks lack the ordered elegance of pinkfeet on the wing.

At Langham I turned north, a downhill detour towards Morston and the coast, through wheat fields where I've countless times seen brents, where I thought the birds I'd just seen might be feeding. Still nothing. I struggled back uphill, a grey partridge grinding gears in a field beside me and, overhead, a buzzard's sorry wail.

Reaching Binham again, I thought I'd altogether failed to find the brents; but east of the priory, looking on the sunlit ribcage of the ruined quire, I caught a movement as I stopped to sip bitter coffee from my flask. Geese were pouring, like a plughole vortex, to the field behind my aunt and uncle's family home, only 200 metres from where I stood. I pedalled there and hid behind the hedge, peering through a gap. The geese seemed settled, so I felt into my panniers for my scope and tripod.

I scanned the flock just once from right to left, seeing a single pale-belly among them and a hybrid brant. Moments later, a shambling man appeared along the lane, dressed in a red-checked shirt. Noting but ignoring me, he walked onto the field and up its grassy headland, towards the geese. Brents are confiding birds, greatly more than pinkfeet, but every black neck in the field went up. The geese walked calmly away, over a flinty ridge. The farmer followed, waving his white handkerchief. This was enough: the birds took flight, filling the chilly day with sound. They circled, trying several times to land again, but red-checked man stood resolute. The geese flew on.

I cycled homewards, onto the glacial mound embracing Binham to the south. As I looked back on the sunlit Benedictine priory – on more than nine centuries of community here – a ball of distant geese arrived from the southwest. I followed with binoculars until they dipped behind the barn-like nave, into a field where hundreds more were plucking at winter wheat. The Warham Road: that was where they'd gone, and where the brant would surely be. No matter. I was tired, with ten more miles to go.

Saturday 26th December

Colder weather came for Christmas, and with it the last of Norfolk's winter geese. Yesterday four taiga bean geese were seen along the River Yare, and this morning there are six.

The Meaning of Geese

The taiga bean goose is an animal of imposing beauty. Like the tundra bean, which I have several times seen this winter, the taiga bean is brown-necked, with a grey-brown back, each feather neatly edged in silver-white. It is by structure that taiga and tundra beans may be identified. The tundra bean goose is a thick-necked, solid bird, its deep bill making it heavy-faced. The taiga bean likewise has a thick neck and a deep bill, but both are conspicuously longer, bestowing a swan-necked grace not shared by other native geese. Often a taiga bean has more yellow-orange in the bill than a tundra, especially along the cutting edge, though this is by no means diagnostic.

Taiga bean geese are unique in personality too; wariest of our wild geese, and the most elusive. Among the few in Norfolk who know them well is Ben Lewis, a warden at the RSPB's Yare Valley Marshes, including Strumpshaw, Buckenham and Cantley. Ben grew up counting dark-bellied brent geese around Foulness in Essex, where his father is local coordinator of the British Trust for Ornithology's Wetland Birds Survey. Ten years ago Ben moved to the Broads, and to his job with the RSPB. His winters, ever since, have been loud with the calls of pinkfeet, whitefronts and taiga beans.

When I spoke to Ben ten days ago, he had just surveyed the marsh, as he does on his birthday every year. He had found no taiga beans. With our climate changing fast and the dwindling West European population of taigas no longer needing to hop the Channel to escape midwinter cold, we both feared this might be the first winter in a century in which no taiga bean geese came to Norfolk. Happily, for one year more, we were wrong.

This winter around 2,000 pinkfeet have been seen along the Yare, far more than would have been expected when Ben arrived. As at Holkham, the Yare flock of Russian whitefronted geese has been broadly stable over these ten winters, except for one when the whitefronts returning to North Warren in Suffolk found the grass too long. They shifted to Buckenham, doubling the flock.

But the taiga bean geese – those winter spirits of the Yare, whose only English flock has been known here since the 1920s – have steadily declined.

Even for the wardens in the Yare, much about these handsome birds remains a mystery. 'We don't really know what taigas eat,' Ben told me, 'though they like the rougher, rushier areas of the marsh. If you go anywhere near them, they just suddenly disappear. I think they hide in vegetation before they fly.'

'I tend to think of them as a mythical goose,' he said, his love for the birds written across his young, dark-bearded face. 'You can scan the whole place and they're not there; and then five paces on you see them. In fact my method for finding them is to scan and then walk twenty paces. The only way to see them well,' he chuckled, 'is to dress from top to toe in hi-vis and walk along the railway line in the open. They seem not to mind when humans behave in predictable ways.

'Taiga beans are very special, but the past few years we've asked: will they return? I often describe it as a sensible thing, not travelling further than they have to nowadays. Perhaps we may see small groups in harsh weather in the future. Older birds may still find their way to Buckenham. They're so interesting compared to other geese. It will be sad to see them go.'

I grew up watching taiga bean geese almost every winter by the Yare, sometimes in their hundreds. I would love to see the last six Norfolk taiga beans this winter but almost certainly I shall not. The Yare is much too far for me to visit on my bike. It is enough to know that, as I write, the orange-patterned bills of taiga bean geese are plucking Buckenham's grass. One winter more.

2021

JANUARY

what tales of Arctic tundras or of temperate lakes

The year begins with a curious bean goose visiting Blakeney. A charming wildfowler warmly teaches me about his craft and his love of geese. We agree that more unites us than divides us. By the month's end, pinkfeet are already leaving, while brent flocks roam more widely across North Norfolk.

Saturday 2nd January

We live in the sky in North Norfolk, on the wind, with the tide. These are our elements, framing the land and our lives. This morning, through an unforgiving winter sky, I cycled sixteen miles to Blakeney: a seaward band of barely blue pressed down on me by layers of cloud like buckled sheets of steel.

    I had packed my panniers, readied my bike, and was leaving for Docking when Mark Golley sent a photo of a most intriguing bean goose he had found with pinks on Blakeney Freshes. Changing my plans, I headed east instead, hoping to see his goose.

The Meaning of Geese

Northeast of Thursford, where the northmost digit of Swanton Great Wood just juts across the A148 – where I once stopped at the Crawfish pub to watch a honey buzzard low above the road – you leave the upper catchment of the Stiffkey. Entering the Glaven catchment, you glimpse the North Sea six miles to the north. Countless times I've seen a change in weather here; often from thick fog on the Stiffkey side to sharp light in the Glaven. Today's cold wind picked up a little as I passed; and more so still when I turned north, and seawards, towards Langham.

Heading down to Blakeney, past banks of winter-glossy alexanders, always feels to me like going home. This is where my father and his siblings were born and grew, children of the village doctor. From here their horses bore them round the local lanes and farms. One village to the east, at Cley, in early summer 1952, legendary warden Billy Bishop showed my father Norfolk's first little egret. I saw several little egrets today. They are widespread now, thanks to ever milder winters.

I saw geese too, my first of 2021. North of the Glaven sluice on Blakeney Freshes, a dozen dark-bellied brent geese grazed, close to a herd of mute swans, their long necks bent together in conspiracy. While I chained my bike to the wooden fence, hundreds of pinkfeet arrived from the west, swirling to the next field north, joining many hundreds already on the marsh. I cursed. This morning Mark had found his bean goose in a group of just two hundred pinks. It would be harder by far to spot among these thousands.

Finding the bird was sadly easy. There was a pheasant shoot in the woods surrounding Wiveton Hall. Every time a gun went off the fearful geese all raised their necks. I quickly saw Mark's lovely bean goose, its slender bill contrasting with the stubby, dark-based bills of pinkfeet all around it.

When Mark sent his photo this morning, he did not offer an identification; nor at the time did we discuss it. The goose in the photo was a young bird, from 2020, its face and bill just right for a taiga bean goose – right enough for me to change my plans and cycle east to Blakeney – but its neck looked short and thick to me, more typical of a tundra bean.

Seeing the goose in life, I studied it with care. Taiga beans are hugely rarer in pinkfoot flocks than tundras; hardly ever seen away from regular winter sites in East Norfolk and in Scotland. Like every bean, this goose had a dark back, though blotched untidily, as it was moulting into adult plumage. Its neck was longer than those of pinkfeet standing round it, and stronger too, but lacked the grace expected in a taiga bean. Its bill and legs, though, clearly hinted taiga. Both were the yellow-orange of butternut squash; the bill marked only by a black nail at its tip, otherwise altogether lacking blacks and browns. More interesting was the structure of the bill: long and slender, with a shallow, straight-edged lower mandible, without a tundra bean's aggressive snarl.

Just as Mark appeared at the sluice, a few minutes' walk away, a light plane passed low above the marsh, followed by more gunshots from the wood. The geese took off in panic. I cursed again; but the birds, still full from feeding under last night's gravid moon, knew that the marsh was safe, and settled quickly. Mark reached me as they did.

'There's the bird,' he said, 'just below the buzzard on the fencepost.' I panned left fast, until I reached the desolate-looking buzzard and found Mark's goose again. For both of us, the bird's bill pointed to a young taiga bean goose, in structure and in colour. So too the colour of its legs. Yet we both felt that its neck was rather stout, except occasionally when a gun went off and all the geese raised their heads in fear.

A barn owl popped onto the ledge of its triangular nestbox on the marsh, seeking midwinter sun. I shivered, eyes smarting in the wind, while Mark and I shared thoughts on the heritage of this beautiful bean goose. For much of the time it rested, even as pinkfeet bustled by. It had only recently arrived, perhaps, from who knows where, and needed sleep.

Later, through sixteen homeward miles, my legs worked hard. My mind worked too, pondering the nature of a vagrant goose. Most likely we shall never know its real identity, nor the path it took before reaching Norfolk. Such mysteries are why I watch and shiver and think and write: awed as I am by the immensity of the natural world.

Sunday 3rd January

During more than two years of my closest friend Sarah's illness, we walked innumerable miles together, along lanes and abandoned railway lines, and we talked. Later, as my friend grew weaker, we went instead to the duckpond at Blakeney where – to our enormous amusement – I tried to teach her the names of all the ducks and geese kept by the Blakeney Wildfowlers Association. I struggle with pinioned birds – deliberately disabled to prevent their flying away – but Sarah and I cherished the hours we spent together here, sitting on the seawall, watching ducks; laughing when I upbraided her for misidentifying a ringed teal, as she always did. She recalled these duck days in the address she wrote to be read at her funeral.

January

Above all, Sarah loved the nēnēs, or Hawaiian geese. Each time we visited the pond, the geese would walk towards the fence to greet us, reaching forward with their buffy, ruffled necks, calling sorrowfully. During one of Sarah's long courses of chemotherapy, I spoke to the Blakeney Wildfowlers, who kindly shared the combination for the padlock on the gate. Next time we went, to her surprise, I smuggled Sarah into the enclosure, to meet her nēnē friends. I have a beautiful photo from that day: her head wrapped in a pale blue scarf, a thoughtful smile on her lips and in her eyes, a nēnē nibbling at her fingers.

In the middle of the twentieth century, the nēnē famously almost vanished from the world. Peter Scott learned of its desperate rarity in the 1930s. In the hope of collaborating in the goose's conservation, he wrote to Herbert Shipman, who kept many of the surviving birds in his garden on Hawai'i. In *The Eye of the Wind*, his autobiography, Scott explains that Shipman promised him a pair of geese, provided he would go to Hawai'i to collect them, an agreement which was thwarted by the outbreak of the Second World War.

After the war, following the establishment of the Severn Wildfowl Trust, Scott sent curator John Yealland to Hawai'i, to assist with a captive breeding programme for the goose. Yealland returned to Slimbridge in 1950 with the promised pair of nēnēs from Herbert Shipman. The following spring both birds laid eggs. 'We sent an urgent cable to Hawaii for a gander,' Scott writes, 'and meanwhile took away the infertile eggs, blew them, ate the contents in an omelette and preserved the shells.' A week later, a male nēnē was sent from Hawai'i. The following spring both females bred successfully and the Wildfowl and Wetlands Trust's role in the recovery of the nēnē began.

Thousands of Hawaiian geese now live in captivity across the world, most of them descended from the founding birds at Slimbridge. In its native range the nēnē is still considered vulnerable by BirdLife International. Many of the 2,500 birds inhabiting the major islands of the chain are of captive origin and have not themselves bred in the wild. The only significant breeding colony is on Kaua'i, in the far north of the islands, where more than two-thirds of all wild birds are found.

Cycling home from the Freshes yesterday, having seen Mark's bean goose among pinks, I took a detour past Blakeney Quay, to give Sarah's love to her nēnē friends. The geese were by the water's edge, their necks like walking sticks, a pose peculiar to these gentle birds. I did not stop, or call them to the fence, but cycled on, glancing to the seawall where many times I sat with my dearest Sarah, and scolded her for muddling pochard, wigeon and ferruginous ducks.

Tuesday 5th January

As a child I announced to my parents that I wanted to be vegetarian. This long-held conviction was permitted at last when I left home for university. I later became vegan. It therefore might seem odd that, for an hour and a half today, I had an engaging conversation with a wildfowler about our common love of geese and of the marshes that they haunt, at the end of which we warmly agreed that our relationship with nature was fundamentally the same.

I had meant to meet Kevin Thatcher on the marsh which Wells and District Wildfowlers Association rents from the Holkham Estate but, as news came last night of another national lockdown, we chose instead to speak by Zoom.

January

Kevin has shot for sixty years, since he was ten years old, and for many of those was chair of Wells Wildfowlers, for whom he now acts as vice president. His is a passion not only for wildfowl and their habitat, but also for the tradition of wildfowling. A longshoreman, he calls himself, one of a dwindling lineage.

I told him – quite sincerely – that I wished to understand, and to describe as fairly as I could, what geese and ducks have meant to him over so many years. 'It's often imagined,' he began by telling me, 'that shooting people like the idea of killing; but killing is only a tiny part of wildfowling. Wildfowlers have a phenomenal respect and admiration, not just for their quarry but for the whole environment. It gets in your blood.

'Wildfowlers have always led the way in conservation. We have a particular affinity for the foreshore and marshes. We took them on when no one else was interested. In many cases clubs took over marshes and protected them from being used as dumps, as they often were. They were Tom Tiddler's land.

'We come from all walks of life. I've shot with professors, airline pilots and car park attendants. Many of the fishing families in Wells are wildfowlers. I once met a wizened old wildfowler on a seawall and grunted in greeting. Coming back, we met again. She took off her hat and I saw she was a blonde young woman. She was a model, a very well-known one. All sorts of people are wildfowlers.'

Kevin was clearly most animated by the history and the craft of wildfowling: the knowledge acquired over lifetimes and over generations. He has canvasses left at the East Lighthouse by Peter Scott when he went to war, which were finished by Kenzie Thorpe, the skilled wildfowler and countryman whom Scott left in charge of his captive geese.

The Meaning of Geese

Kevin also possesses decoys brought to the lighthouse by Van Campen Heilner – US adventurer, writer and hunter – which Scott repainted to represent European birds. 'It's not a sport; it's a way of life. We pit ourselves against birds in their element. We have to understand the tides, the weather, the moon and the birds themselves. I've shot on estuaries all around the UK with old-time wildfowlers: Morecambe Bay, the Humber, the Ribble, Lindisfarne. Talking to them you feel that connection, that sense of history, of belonging in these wild places.'

Kevin and I were getting on well. Here was a man whose ethics and lifestyle I could readily respect; but I felt obliged to raise the issue which most troubles me. Geese pair for life. Friends have told me of heartbreaking encounters with lone geese, flying between fields in which flocks had been feeding, calling constantly, searching – apparently – for lost partners. Several times this winter I've seen the same. When I spoke to artist Jonathan Yule in September he told me a story which had been instrumental in his own decision to give up shooting geese. One morning, in his days as a shepherd near Docking, he had just moved store lambs from one harvested beet field to another. 'A big lot of geese had gone off at 7:30 when I'd arrived,' he said. 'As I went round the field, rolling up the three-strand electric wire, I was accompanied by a single goose flying round and round, craning its neck to look down.

'In the middle of the field I found the body of a dead goose, still warm. I was convinced the field was the last place the lone goose had seen its partner alive. It was a poignant moment, knowing the goose at my feet had died a slow and painful death, after taking a pellet out of range from an inexpert wildfowler.'

January

I asked Kevin how he could honour the thread of his community, keeping alive the memory and lore of wildfowlers past, while severing the thread of a goose's life, its pair bond, and the ancestral knowledge carried in its flock and genes.

He did not dodge the question. 'I can't say I don't bother about it. I don't know. It's so hard to explain: killing the very thing I admire. The way we look at it, we become almost part of their migration.' He thought for a while. 'The peregrine has no choice but to kill. It's an instinct. It becomes an instinct for us too. It becomes part of your life. When there's a moon and a north wind and the windowpanes are rattling you're driven to be out.'

I understood the meaning of this kindly, eloquent man. My thoughts went to *The Book of Merlyn*. When Arthur's flock of white-fronted geese leaves Lincolnshire, bound for the Russian Arctic, White writes of the lone birdcatcher on the marsh and the love he has for the very birds he kills: '...for he stood still solemnly, and took off his hat. He did this every spring religiously, when the wild geese left him, and every autumn, when he saw the first returning gaggle.'

Saturday 9th January

After several days of dishwater gloom and northern cold, today I wanted brents in sunshine, and the warm burr of their voices. I cycled to the football pitch beside the quay at Wells. Here, to my surprise, there were no geese. Just molehill-dappled grass and icy tarmac, which pulled my wheels from under me as, gingerly, I turned onto the road to Holkham.

The Meaning of Geese

In Holkham village, there were geese. I saw the greylags by the roadside first, their sunlit orange bills like triangles of Leicester cheese. Behind them, stealing grazing from a portly group of rams, hundreds of pinkfeet wove across the winter-punished grass; and in the nearest corner of the paddock two Egyptian geese, alone and puffed with pride.

A young marsh harrier – last year's chick – dawdled above the grazing marsh beyond, its lazy poise belying fell intent. Wigeon sprang up in silvery flocks at its approach, and brent geese too, muttering in alarm. The geese circled towards me, revealing among them a dozen barnacles, the black-white-black of tails and backs shining in the morning's welcome light. Many of the brent geese landed in the paddock with the pinkfeet, forming a dense, black slick between them. The barnacles flew north again, to vanish in the marsh.

Sixty years ago, when Kevin Thatcher began wildfowling, the dark-bellied brent goose was 'the wildest of the wild,' a bird found only on remote coastal saltmarshes and mudflats. Brents were numerically rare then too, their population having collapsed in the 1930s, following mass die-offs of eelgrass, their favoured winter food. 'There was a romance about them,' Kevin told me, 'these geese which nested in Siberia, where nuclear testing was taking place.'

In 1954 the brent goose was granted strict protection from hunting in the UK; and in the 1970s the bird – which wildfowlers regarded as a shy companion along the shore, and ecologists thought would feed only in the intertidal zone – effected a dramatic behavioural change. From January 1970, flocks of brent geese were observed feeding inland of Essex seawalls, in fields of grass and winter wheat. By the mid-1970s the number of inland-feeding brents had risen steeply, both in the UK and the Netherlands. Brent geese still commonly feed on arable fields today, though only after a few weeks spent in saltmarsh when they first arrive. Sometimes they roam as far as eight miles from the coast, even to the village by the River Stiffkey where I grew up.

Having watched the brents and pinks at length, I cycled on, along the north wall of the park, stopping near the turning south to Peterstone, to scan the marsh for whitefronts. I saw a distant group of feral Canadas first, my sixth goose of the day; then, straining through binoculars to pick up birds the best part of a mile away, I found a huddle of neat, dark whitefronts, dwarfed by burly greylags all around them. Andy tells me 220 whitefronts have now arrived. Then, thrillingly, I saw a male marsh harrier in display above a strip of tawny reed, hurling himself chest-first into each rapturous dive, promising spring with every rasping shriek.

I heard a truck pull up behind me. 'You stand out a mile,' said a familiar voice, in friendly mockery of my old red bike. It was Jake Fiennes, Holkham's director of conservation, a thick fleece hat pulled low onto his brow. We shared our news across the road, not having seen each other since before the geese returned. 'The two snow geese are with the pinkfoot flock,' Jake said in parting. 'If you go up to Burnham Thorpe, they've just landed in a wheat field.' So I cycled home through Thorpe; but all the many pinks I saw were on the wing.

Sunday 10th January

My goose-watching has altogether changed now. Our lockdown lives are – appropriately – much restricted. The sole permitted reason to be out by bike is exercise. I still have binoculars around my neck, and briefly stop by fields to scan for geese, but I no longer take a telescope. With lockdown predicted to last until well into February – long after the bulk of our pinkfeet will have left – it seems I have watched my last significant flock of pinks this winter.

Instead I cycle through a landscape occupied by geese, watching the way they move across it, hurtling along muddy lanes in a vain attempt to follow their noisy airborne flocks. Increasingly, I also witness signs of spring. Just south of Wells today I spun round in the road on seeing a tiny galaxy of precocious blackthorn blooms. Nearby, a woodpigeon teetered on a mound of ivy, guzzling its plump black berries: equally a sign of longer days to come. In Holkham village, east of Lady Anne's Drive, hundreds of brent geese grazed, until four Egyptian geese – their hormones primed for squabbling and for breeding – flew in and barged between them, necks back and shoulders spread, flashing snow-white coverts. The brents politely raised their collared necks, startled by all this unsought clamour, and returned to feeding.

Yesterday, when I texted Andy about the twelve barnacles I had seen, he told me that the flock which has wintered at Burnham Overy for the past few years had arrived some weeks ago, numbering 120 birds. 'They always turn up in November,' he wrote, 'and depart about February. I don't think they're the birds that breed in the park, but Kane's ringing next year might prove otherwise. The park birds disappear in August and start to return from February to April. It would be nice to think the Burnham Overy birds were genuinely wild winter visitors. They've certainly been building year on year.'

I was keen to see these barnacles today, and cycled west along the north edge of the park again, smelling the warm

January

tang of a fox where it had jumped the wall. Just as I arrived at Whincover, the mud track leading north to Burnham Overy Dunes, two kites flew low above the marsh, greylags and curlews springing into flight ahead of them, and dunlin shimmering in a tight flock across a flood. I stood, in cutting cold, and searched, but saw no barnacles.

Heading home, I stopped a moment by the track to Marsh Farm, which perches above Burnham Overy Marshes. In the misty distance, through a gappy hedge, I made out half a dozen barnacle geese. Here, then, was the flock, hidden from view by aged hawthorns. Like Andy, I wondered where they came from, these lovely geese; what tales of Arctic tundras or of temperate lakes were carried in their genes. Musing on this I cycled twelve miles home, the shrill winter voices of the pinkfeet all around me tempered by gargling rooks, gathered at their breeding woods anew. For spring comes.

Friday 15th January

The drum of a great spotted woodpecker hammers hope into a naturalist's heart. Leaning on the steel fence of ruined St Margaret's church in West Raynham today, I heard my first of spring.

Despite the raw, wet cold of January, the bird's tattoo was heartening. So too a blue tit's springtime chiming from the avenue of limes along the road. I had cycled the short distance to West Raynham to see a greylag goose, which my dear friend David Stubbs has been watching in his local flock since New Year's Day. It has an orange collar, bearing the black letters PAP. When David first texted me photographs, I sent them on to Kane – thinking the greylag might have been ringed by the Wildfowl and Wetlands Trust – but he suggested the British Trust for Ornithology instead: to report the sighting and learn what was known of the goose's life.

PAP was ringed in July 2019, in a moulting flock of greylags 22 miles to the south at Cranwich, in the Brecks. It was not sexed at the time and was seen just once more at the site, the following month. It had not been reported again, until – some 18 months later – David found it by Raynham Lake at the start of this year. He has seen it there every day since, with around 350 other greylags.

As I arrived today, and leaned my bike against the back wall of the village reading room, the geese were almost all asleep, including PAP. When the bird woke up it wove along the back flank of the flock, neck almost always raised: on edge it seemed, with the mien of an unpaired gander, searching – perhaps – for a partner, or simply a familiar goose.

A collared goose inspires conflicting thoughts in me. The feathers of PAP's neck were ruffled where its collar pushed down on them. Most likely no one knows how much this affects a goose's temperature regulation, or its aerodynamics in flight. Studies have suggested a collar may sometimes snag a goose's bill, or the bird may struggle to attract a mate because some aspect of its visual identity is altered. Such findings, though, are inconclusive.

From a human point of view, a collar permits a rare and privileged view into a goose's life. Among the many greylags resting and grazing by Raynham Lake today, few were individually recognisable to our eyes. Even were David to spend his whole life watching these geese, learning to identify each pair by tiny details of plumage and personality, his subjective knowledge would be rendered meaningless as soon as the birds

January

dispersed along the Wensum to breed in spring. Wearing a collar, emblazoned with three black letters, legible to anyone birding with a telescope, an individual goose is objectively identifiable. If PAP finds a mate, raises chicks, flies back to Cranwich, or on to somewhere new, its life can be mapped. Unquestionably this is good for our understanding of these geese and how they use the landscape, and ultimately for our ability to protect them.

A common gull padded across the grass close by the flock. Jackdaws were nearby too, moving in noisy bands between the wood and stands of parkland trees. Two roe deer – a doe and last year's slender young – tiptoed from the wood's edge into a field; and trilling long-tailed tits entwined the churchyard trees above our heads.

One other goose was clearly identifiable among David's local flock today: a small and silvery female. Her colour put me in mind of an eastern greylag goose – a form I've seen a thousand times in India, China and Mongolia – and I recalled an email I received a month ago from a local farmer friend. He explained that in the 1970s he had kept a flock of eastern greylags. The geese bred freely and he moved the young to a property he had at Raynham, from where they colonised the lake.

My farmer friend suggested I look for eastern greylags if I were ever passing Raynham on my bike; but all the other birds we saw today were textbook western greylags, with deep-based orange bills and a muddy cast to necks, flanks and saddles, contrasting with their silver shoulders as they flew off from the park. The innumerable western greylags now breeding across Norfolk – themselves descended from birds released by wildfowlers in the 1960s – have swamped the founding bloodline of the Raynham flock. Just this one little female bore the frosted colour of an eastern greylag: reminding me of a farmer's flock and of the degree to which we humans shape the landscape and what we call the wild.

Sunday 17th January

Yesterday it snowed. Not the crisp and even snow of comfortable Christmas fiction, but a thin, wet smear, followed all day by bitter rain. Today was from another world: the Klimt-trunked birches on the common gilt by winter light; the first flowers of European gorse beneath them, coaxed into timid being by the sun. I set off along the Dry Road on my bike.

At this time of year – more so than ever this wet, grey, virus-haunted winter – each sunlit second recovered from the solstice seems a blessing; each hint of spring, however weak, a joy. Two robins sang as I cycled north, antiphonally, across the road: one from a hawthorn hedge, the other from a block of pines. Hearing the first of autumn's robins in July each year, my heart sinks, for it spells the death of summer; but these two sang with the rich, warm tone and long-note coda of robins singing for spring. A dunnock sang too. A pheasant cock giving his scraping crow.

My first geese were at the Crabbe Road junction, where a group of greylags has fed in a weedy field all winter and gathered around a flooded pit. I stopped to look and, to my surprise, saw pinkfeet, nineteen of them, legs candied by the lovely light. Further north, by the Golden Gates, I turned along the south wall of the park, then through the imposing South Gate towards Holkham Hall.

By Repton's remodelled lake I counted greylags, my bike propped nearby against a tree. Just over 150 geese were here, the odd pair splintering from the flocks, spring's hormones overcoming winter's imperative to stay together. I panned from shore to shore, my binoculars lingering on lovely shoveler drakes, their chestnut flanks warm in the day's low sun, and on the liver heads of pochard. Clusters of ashy gadwall drakes quacked breathily to dappled ducks. Coots squeaked.

As most of Holkham's geese are in the grazing marsh I cycled on, turning onto the coast road at the Victoria Inn. Not much further to the west, I heard the distant yapping calls of whitefronts, which give them their Norfolk name of laughing goose, and I stopped by a gate to scan the marsh. The geese were flying in small, dark groups – their orange legs blazing in the January sun – and dropping to land beside thick-necked greylags on the grass.

I cycled on again. A water deer bounded across the road, flashing its tawny rump; a hare, behind the mustard-lichened hedge, flattened himself into the snow-wet earth at my approach; and pinkfeet flew inland above me. Holkham's pinkfoot roost is dwindling now. Typically, in our climate-changing world, Norfolk's flocks have largely left for Lancashire and Scotland by January's end. Some will linger into February, as they have my whole life here, but already the robin's coda and the gorse's yellow blooms announce the end of winter's pinkfoot days.

Monday 18th January

There might easily have been no pinkfeet in North Norfolk at all. As David Lyles told me on his farm in late October, the geese abandoned their roosts at Wells and Holkham altogether following the Second World War, when artillery along the coast drove them to the Wash. Though from the

1960s, as sugar beet cultivation spread, pinkfeet returned to feed around David's farm at Muckleton, it was not until the start of the 1980s that a few birds came back to roost at Holkham. And it was the Wells Wildfowlers who ensured they stayed.

When I spoke to Kevin Thatcher recently, he told me that wildfowlers had always held wild geese in the highest regard. Prior to massive population increases in UK greylags and Icelandic pinkfeet in the second half of the twentieth century, and the move inland of brent geese from the 1970s, geese were both wary and rare. 'Geese were unattainable,' Kevin told me. 'When I was a boy, we would spend five days in a tent in Scotland and get one goose and just sit and look at it – not even wanting to pluck it – as if it was a religious object.'

Kevin shot one of the first pinkfeet which returned to Wells in the early 1980s. 'We realised straight away that the pinks would come back. We saw them building up.' However, given the high status of wild geese among shooting people, professional guides quickly cashed in, bringing clients from across the country to shoot them as they fed on tenant farms around the Holkham Estate. Kevin, then chair of Wells Wildfowlers, and his friends were alarmed for the birds' future. 'A lot of people came up after geese; so we went to see the late Lord Leicester, Eddie, who was our president at the time. Straight away he asked us what we wanted him to do. We told him we would give the geese full protection at their roosts, if he would protect them on the land. He wrote a letter then and there, to all his tenants, forbidding shooting geese on their farms.'

Kevin was keen I understood the deep concern that wildfowlers have for their quarry and for the landscape they inhabit. 'Our bylaws go above and beyond national laws. We establish refuge areas ourselves. The birds need two things: to roost in peace and feed in peace. Wildfowling has a very long apprenticeship. We get to know the birds incredibly well because a mistake is a criminal offence. Individually you can be prosecuted, or have your gun taken away, but you have a responsibility to the club too.'

The timely action of the wildfowlers enabled pinkfeet to re-establish themselves at Wells and Holkham, allowing new generations of North Norfolk people to know the thrill of watching as they fly to roost. Allowing me to immerse myself in their ever-changing flocks this cold, grey winter long.

Not all experiences among pinkfeet are transcendent, though. 'I once shot a goose from behind the beach huts.' Kevin told me, laughing at the recollection. 'A bloke shot out from a hut with no trousers on, followed by a half-naked woman.'

Tuesday 19th January

I first met Professor Debbie Pain on a snow-covered mountainside in Ladakh one bitter February day, where she and her husband Duncan were watching two young snow leopards as they waited on a distant ledge for their mother to return. At the time she was director of conservation at the Wildfowl and Wetlands Trust, though she has since retired. 'Retirement,' she told me when we spoke by Zoom today, 'means working forty hours a week rather than sixty. You work just as hard but choose what you do. You also have the liberty of saying what you want, to whom you want, as you're only representing yourself. It's rather liberating!'

The Meaning of Geese

In November, the European Parliament voted to ban the use of lead ammunition in wetlands across the EU; a momentous step for wildlife, towards which Debbie and many colleagues have been working for decades. Her scientific career began almost forty years ago, with a doctoral thesis on the biochemistry of lead poisoning in birds, both from gunshot and from petrol, which at the time was routinely leaded. Ever since, she has been gravely concerned about the effects of lead ammunition on bird and human health; and committed to removing it from the environment and the human food chain.

Lead gunshot gets into birds by ingestion, Debbie explained. 'About 5,000 tonnes of lead shot are used in the UK each year,' she told me, 'some 2,000 tonnes for game shooting and 3,000 for target shooting. Each cartridge contains around 300 individual pellets of lead, most of which never hit a bird.' Thus, billions of tiny pellets are deposited in the environment every year. It can take decades or centuries for them to degrade. They sink more quickly in soft soils, but can be brought back to the surface, or buried deeper, when soils are disturbed by agriculture.

'Ducks, geese and swans mostly ingest lead shot in winter during shooting season,' Debbie said, 'when it is available on the soil surface. They probably mistake it for food or for the particles of grit they eat to help grind food.' Even though, since 1999, lead ammunition has been banned in England for shooting waterfowl and over designated wetlands, such as Sites of Special Scientific Interest and the foreshore, lead shot remains a significant problem for geese, as they routinely forage on farmland where it is legally used to shoot pheasants and partridges.

'Lead is quite a soft metal and is easily abraded by grit in waterfowl gizzards. It is then dissolved by stomach acids and absorbed through the intestine wall, entering the blood. From the blood it concentrates in the liver, kidneys and bones. It's incredibly toxic,' Debbie told me. The source of lead is irrelevant, she says, and the toxin is unusual in that there is no minimum threshold below which you cannot detect effects. Once ingested, lead suppresses the production of blood enzymes, especially one called ALAD which is necessary for haemoglobin production, so birds with chronic exposure can become anaemic.

Birds that eat enough shot can very quickly die of acute poisoning. Others, though, die more slowly, after eating and retaining just a few pellets of lead. These chronically poisoned birds tend to die of starvation over several weeks. An estimated 50,000 to 100,000 waterfowl die of lead poisoning in the UK each year. Across Europe the figure is one million. Around three times as many are affected by sublethal doses, which can affect their immune systems, coordination and behaviour, making them more likely to be shot, and more likely to contract infections.

Lead affects predators, scavengers and, in consequence, whole ecosystems too. To explore its wider impacts, Debbie and her colleagues studied buzzards which had been found dead. 'There are four stable isotopes of lead,' she said, 'and their proportions vary with the source of lead, each having a particular fingerprint; so we were able to demonstrate that much of the lead in dead buzzard tissues was probably from ingestion of shot.' The peak of lead in buzzard livers comes in winter, when pheasants are being shot and buzzards scavenging them. Even sublethal doses are a concern. In a recent study in Sweden, scientists found that the flight height and movement rate of golden eagles tagged with transmitters seemed to be affected when they had even slightly elevated levels of blood lead.

The Meaning of Geese

The impacts of lead shot in the human food chain were once ignored, as it was thought that any gunshot we ingested passed rapidly through our guts; but here again Debbie and her team found evidence to the contrary. 'We purchased shot gamebirds and cooked them. We were able to show that gunshot often fragmented on impact, leaving minute particles in the meat.' After removing whole or easily visible fragments of shot, they found that average lead concentration in gamebird meat was twelve times that permitted in the EU for domestic meats, like chicken and beef.

Happily, attitudes are changing. In February 2020, nine major UK shooting and landowner organisations agreed they would like to see an end to the use of lead ammunition in shotguns for shooting wild game over the next five years.

'And now we have the EU regulation banning lead gunshot in wetlands too,' Debbie told me with enthusiasm. 'I have been working on this since 1991 when the IWRB [now Wetlands International] held a workshop, attended by scientists, shooters and others from across the world. It concluded that the only solution, to protect wildfowl, was to stop using lead gunshot in wetlands, and replace it with non-toxic shot. We have been advocating this change ever since. I've always been led by the science. From my perspective, this has never been an attack on shooting, but rather an attack on avoidable poisoning.'

In spite of Debbie's cheerful nature, our conversation had been deeply sobering. To change the mood, I asked what geese had meant to her, over a career spent watching and protecting birds. Her face lit up as she told me of Christmases spent at Caerlaverock on the Solway, among great swirling flocks of barnacle geese visiting from Svalbard.

January

Then – a smile breaking across her lovely face – she remembered an incident from her PhD: 'I used to catch Canada geese in Hyde Park in London, and in Yorkshire, to compare their blood lead in the days of leaded petrol. Once, when I was drawing blood from a bird in Yorkshire, someone jogged my elbow and I injected Canada goose blood into my hand, hitting an artery with the needle.'

Her hand aching, Debbie visited a laconic Yorkshire GP, to ask whether she should worry. Administering a tetanus booster, he gravely shook his head. 'You want to keep an eye on that,' he said, 'in case you wake up going honk.'

Wednesday 20th January

On a visit to Snettisham in September, I saw a goose I cannot forget. As I stumbled through the first light into the coming day, greylags were beginning to fly inland to feed. Later, pinkfeet followed from their roost on the mud of the Wash. In wait for them, behind the seawall, there were wildfowlers. Throughout the first hour of the day, the hard crack of their guns could be heard.

I saw the goose much later, on the walk back from watching Snettisham's mesmerising flocks of knot. Alone and dazed, among a happy crowd of mallards, it was a greylag. Raw blood streamed from its bill and through the once-white feathers of its vent, as it waited for an agonising death.

Wildfowlers are my fellow conservationists – of this I have no doubt – and I honour the knowledge that they have of wild places and their commitment to them. For my part, though, the firing of hot steel or tungsten at enormous speed, with intent to smash bone and muscle, is an act of violence I shall never understand.

The Meaning of Geese

The ornithologist and author W. H. Hudson, who often visited Wells and Holkham in the years before the First World War, must have been exceptional in his day, for he felt similarly about the Norfolk geese he loved. In *Adventures Among Birds*, published in 1913, he tells an avid gentleman hunter that a wild goose is 'so intelligent a bird that it would be like shooting at a human being.'

He also declines to buy a pink-footed goose which he is offered in Wells. 'I could only reply that it was indeed a fine bird, and I congratulated my old friend on his luck, but I wasn't buying a goose... I would as soon eat a lark, or a quail, or a nice plump young individual of my own species as this wise and noble bird.'

In *The Eye of the Wind*, Peter Scott recounts his own slow realisation that he no longer wished to kill wild geese. It began on a spring day in 1932, when he and a friend shot twenty-three greylags. Two of the birds survived and, as soon as Scott had them in his hands, he wanted to nurture them back to health. They recovered and he kept them for many years. Later, following the Second World War, he tells of the goose which altogether changed his heart and mind. It had been left to die on a sandbank, after a day's shooting had broken both its legs. Seeing the goose, still alive, the following morning, Scott questioned his right to cause such suffering, famously remarking that he would not wish such a fate on a sworn enemy.

He sold his guns and did not shoot again, becoming one of history's most passionate advocates for waterfowl conservation and for wetlands. In a poignant passage from early in *The Eye of the Wind*, this celebrated wildfowler – writer of treasured books on the sport – describes showing a wildfowler around the pens at Slimbridge. As snow geese fly low above their heads, the sportsman remarks that he could easily knock some of them down. 'When those same Snow Geese landed at our feet' Scott writes, 'and walked up to feed from my hand I could sense that he was very much ashamed of the remark.'

Friday 22nd January

I cycled south today, away from the marshes and sea, for the first time since this season with geese of mine began. I was bound instead for the woods, as the sky was bright, after three more days of rain and punishing wind, and I had a bird to see.

It took me years to twig that goshawk meant goose-hawk. Only on hearing a US scientist pronounce gosling with the unvoiced S we use in goshawk, did the penny drop. For W. B. Lockwood, however, in *The Oxford Book of British Bird Names*, goshawk is a misnomer, which probably refers to the peregrine, a bird he considered more likely to be used against geese.

The first bird to which I lifted my binoculars when I reached the wood today was a female goshawk in display. A goshawk is death with feathers, a formidable hunter, recorded taking everything from grasshoppers to capercaillie, and filmed crashing demonically through trees in pursuit of squirrels. Were I a woodland bird, a goshawk would be my greatest fear. But in territorial display a goshawk has a balletic grace which belies its predatory lust. This morning's female soared above a block of dull green pines, giving the slow and purposeful flaps which signal she intends to nest.

Five red deer hinds materialised from the wood's edge as I watched, their toffee rumps warm in the morning's light. Though hundreds of metres away, I was upwind of them, and every time they caught my scent their muzzles turned accusingly towards me.

A lone greylag flew across the far south corner of the wood, reminding me of geese. My frigid toes could stand the cold no more and I cycled on to Binham, my slender shadow flickering northwards on the tarmac, like a compass needle. There were no brents at Binham, nor at Wighton, that I could find, but nearing the pink cottages on the Walsingham to Barsham road I found them grazing in the wet dip of a field of winter wheat. This was the flock in which, before the current lockdown, friends had been seeing the same black brant I saw in November near Wells.

I counted the flock from left to right and right to left, each time seeing just over a hundred birds; until one, in the middle, moved its neck and I caught the clergyman collar of the brant. It turned, revealing its peat-black body and bold white flank: as handsome as when I saw it last.

Soon though I was distracted from the geese, as a hen harrier blew along the back hedge of the field, its rusted tones identifying it as a first-year bird. A Norfolk naturalist's life is only an allotted number of hen harriers long, and seeing these paperscrap birds is always joy.

Hares scuffled in the crop behind the harrier, a female beating off a male's hormonal suit. Tomorrow grey skies and snow are due, but today has been blessed by sun, by hares, by larks, by geese, and by a brute-chested female goshawk above a wood.

Monday 25th January

While much of the country lies sheathed in snow, in North Norfolk for the past two nights we have had frost. Last

January

winter was absurdly mild here, with no more than six nights of freezing weather, but this winter has already more than doubled that. For days now the village pond outside my door has been frozen hard, but for the far end where the warmth and bustle of forty ducks have kept a pool of water open.

In yesterday's pinkish dawn, house sparrows and a starling bickered over the nest-hole in the eaves above my desk, and one of our pond-haunting pairs of herring gulls broke into a peal of unhinged laughter for the first time in 2021. Despite the cold, it felt like spring, so I got my aged bike out of the shed and set off cycling. A mile out I was frightened by ice-crusted puddles in the road and decided I should turn for home.

Today I waited for the noon sun to melt the ungritted tarmac by my house and set off for the coast. I only made it six miles north. Here, in a wheat field, I came across a flock of dark-bellied brents. I pulled into a dirty lay-by, slipped down the bank to the edge of the field and the sun, and quickly counted 500 birds. Among them – but always on the edge – was the neat black brant I saw just half a mile away last week.

In immaculate stripes, thousands of wheat rows crossed the field towards me. Over them the brent flock flowed, its sinuous form at odds with the satellite-drilled precision of the crop. This is the central tension of our landscape: between nature's dynamic and stochastic process and humanity's need to own, to change, to control. We have an island myth that we Britons are nature-lovers, that we – uniquely – cherish the landscape and its wildlife. It is untrue. All around me nature hunkered only in neglected corners, between huge blocks of landscape which – save for their allotted crops – were all but dead.

The Meaning of Geese

Yes, there were redwings, fizzing overhead; and, yes, a kite, foxed by the winter sun, swept in mischief low above the geese, scattering them in a burbling cloud. Yes, woodpigeons courted on a distant power line, the male bird all but losing his foothold as he fanned his preposterous tail and bowed. But for miles to north and east almost all that I could see were intensive fields of single crops.

A happy sky-blue tractor dragged a distant plough, churning the rich North Norfolk earth, haloed by common gulls. I am by no means anti-farming. Three of my grandparents, and my mother, were born on farms. Both of my godfathers, one of them an uncle, are North Norfolk farmers. I love and respect both men. I do not grow my own food, so I rely on farmers to grow it. However, if we are to mend our savaged landscape, and mend ourselves, we must be honest about what we have lost and how.

In the twentieth century – as thousands of miles of ancient hedges were grubbed out, as almost all our farm ponds were filled, as fallow fields were drilled with winter cereals, as tumbledown barns were converted into housing, as nitrate fertilisers destroyed soil biodiversity, and as pesticides killed our insects, birds and annual plants en masse – the UK suffered a catastrophic and closely documented loss of wildlife. More than half of the UK's farmland birds have been lost since 1970, snuffed out by changing land use. Declines in other monitored groups have been comparable and many plants and animals of farmland, scrub, hedges, old commons, orchards and woodland edge – all of which were common in living memory – have been ushered to extinction's waiting room by our actions. Among them nightingale, turtle dove, willow tit, spotted flycatcher, tree sparrow, corn bunting, and lesser spotted woodpecker. Without them we are infinitely poorer.

January

A robin sang, as I gloomily reflected on the loss of wildlife I have witnessed in my lifetime, and a distant greyish wisp solidified into a skein of forty geese, heading towards the flock, and dropping almost silently to join it. They were followed by three groups more – six, twenty and twelve – each arriving from the north, landing into the east, towards me, their charcoal bellies smouldering in the sun. Six hundred geese now fed on cereal shoots before me, perverse beneficiaries of intensive agriculture, of protein-yielding nitrates.

Some geese grazed, some slept, some raised their necks in vigilance. The flock's shape shifted as it moved across the green-striped field: now a circle with an empty centre, now a curving smudge. As each bird turned, its white vent caught the sun and – watched with the naked eye – the whole flock seemed to shimmer like a slo-mo shoal of fish. From time to time a single bird would flap its wings, three-four quick flaps to waken muscles and order wayward feathers. Sometimes a gander jabbed another bird, which tottered forwards, wings lifted in alarm.

I heard a linnet's gravelly note above me in the blue. A single linnet: a stray thread from the great sparrow, finch and bunting flocks which fed on winter stubbles here just seventy years ago, festooning ancient hedges like blankets left to dry. The wind grew crueller as the shadows lengthened and, heart weighty with the landscape's slow, continuing death, I left the geese and pedalled home.

Friday 29th January

I laughed out loud today, in happiness. Cycling coastwards, through the lark-bright sky, I heard, just north of Barsham, the rapturous clatter of a chaffinch from the hedge, defying winter. Just further on, a song thrush shouted from a wiry rank of pines, and laughter toppled from me.

I chained my bike in the woods at Wells and followed the sound of pinkfeet to the marsh. Looking south, to town, Quarles Marsh was backlit by the sun, each ditch-side veil of last year's reed alive with light. Geese crowded round the silvered water: a noisy band of greylags on the near shore, and a flock of pinkfeet on the muddied grass beyond. For weeks, coordinated counts of pinks around the Norfolk coast have been thwarted by cloud and fog, but already large numbers have surely left for Lancashire. When I spoke to Kane this week, he was watching flocks of pinkfeet, from his desk at home in Manchester, as they headed west across the Pennines, having flown inland along the Humber.

I had felt that, thanks to Covid, lockdown and the lengthening days, I had seen the last of pinkfoot flocks this winter; but early this morning Andy texted to say 10,000 were still at Holkham. Here, at the east end of the National Nature Reserve, I could see a tenth of them, mostly asleep, as they'd fed under last night's moon.

Two thousand lapwings got up from the marsh, in waves from east to west. Just as the presence of a black hole can be inferred from the movement of the stars around it, the passage of a peregrine is betrayed by panicked birds above a marsh. Each time the lapwing flocks took flight, flapping on ink-dipped wings, I scanned among them for a falcon. I found a buzzard hunkered on a post, a disapproving magpie on a bush nearby. I found a sparrowhawk, round-shouldered and hungering for a careless pipit. But I could see no peregrine.

January

Eventually I caught her as she sliced along the water's edge and dropped behind a fringe of reed. Hundreds of wigeon lifted from the flood. Time and again she churned the flock, strafing the water in their wake, or switching back to scatter them. A marsh harrier followed, languid and lazy-winged, but no less bent on killing.

A fidget, beside me in the sandy track, caught my attention. Two metres from me, a dunnock was feeding in the open, its left foot clubbed. I feared that moving my binoculars would scare the bird away; but it stayed, and I studied each flawless detail of its feathers: the nut-brown edges to its wings, the down wisps reaching from its flanks onto its mantle, its dry-slate brow and collar. For an hour my mind had reached into the vastness of the marsh, following with fascination the distant drama of a hunting peregrine. Here at my feet a bright-eyed little bird reminded me each brent, each curlew, starling and each wigeon is an individual, a life, a struggle to survive and pass on genes, a story.

Leaving Wells, as I cycled home, I saw a group of pinkfeet hurl themselves out of the sky into a newly harvested field of beet. By the end of January, Norfolk's pinkfeet have essentially retreated to coastal grazing marshes, from which they rarely stray, but one field south of Wells the spoils of frosted January-lifted beet were much too good to miss.

I left my bike in a bed of roadside grass and crept along the hedge until I found a head-height notch in the glossy wall of ivy. The field was full of geese, heads down, picking at the remnants of the crop. Pinkfeet are wary birds but these – with no idea that I was there – fed close to me, the field's flint blues and subtle browns echoed in their plumage. More geese kept coming from the coast: shrill hundreds tumbling in the western wind to land with the most exuberant whiffling that I've seen all winter long. Again I laughed, for joy.

Sunday 31st January

A motley mix of geese I've seen today, not one of them truly native. This morning a dear friend, who is struggling, wanted to talk, so we walked in the valley for two sunlit hours, upriver from where I live. Chaffinch song toppled from the hedges, and roe deer – a doe with leggy twins – retreated to a copse as we approached. I spotted four distant geese, flying along the river towards us, above the purplish line of alders at its edge. Lifting binoculars, I saw the neat black necks of barnacles: a pair with last year's goslings. Minutes later they were followed by three more.

Downriver from where I live is Pensthorpe. Since the park's foundation, more than thirty years ago, a feral flock of barnacle geese has bred around its gravel pits. In April, sometimes, I hear a prospecting pair above my house. The birds we saw this morning were no doubt heading home to Pensthorpe, perhaps from foraging under last night's near-full moon. Feral though they may be, their Arctic genes came, generations back, from Greenland, or Siberia or from Svalbard.

By afternoon the sky was cloudy, and a spiteful northeast wind had come. Cycling was a battle as I headed for the scrape which friends have made along the river, a few miles down from where I live. For a fifth winter Russian white-fronted geese have joined the feral flock of Canadas and greylags here. This week just one young whitefront has been seen, and with it – remarkably – a dark-bellied brent.

January

Norfolk's two roving snow geese are also to be found here. Since arriving on the coast at Holkham in late November, and moving from there to Docking where I saw them last, these escapees have visited the Wensum valley, and the Fens at Terrington. After another recent spell with pinkfeet around Holkham, they're back in the valley now, associating with 600 greylags.

A hundred geese, or so, were by the river when I arrived: greylags, Canadas and Egyptians. Another hundred were in the field behind, where plump brown cattle had ploughed the ground to mud. These, all greylags, were picking through the scraps of fodder left by the farmer for his herd. Hundreds of jackdaws were scrumping here too. From time to time, they billowed upwards in a great black cloud, dropping sharp calls to earth, as if to ground themselves.

Hundreds of teal were feeding round the rush clumps of the scrape, and dozens of wigeon on its grassy bank. A heron sulked beside the water, and – a rare bird here – a liver-headed goosander preened. I was dreaming, lost in the piping music of the teal, when the bullet of an otter broke the water's surface. She dived again, but resurfaced by the opposite bank, the wet muzzle of a second otter with her, her wiry tail tip visible for a second above the water. To my delight, a third snout poked above the frigid water, and three playful otters – a mother and 2020's pups – became a single writhing beast.

They swam upriver, and I lost them, but I deduced their path among the rushes as teal sprang into nimble flight at their approach, and a copper-feathered pheasant burst noisily across the river. More greylags were arriving now, in tens and twenties, complaining in their adenoidal way. I watched each pewter-shouldered group come in to land, hoping to see the snow geese with them. And then I laughed as, in the open among the greylags in the muddy field, I saw them. For all my scanning and rescanning, for all my imagined prowess as a naturalist, I had missed these two white geese as they arrived.

FEBRUARY

a cycling milestone

Greylag geese spread out to their breeding sites across North Norfolk, while remaining pinkfeet retreat to coastal grazing marshes. I pass a cycling milestone: a thousand miles cycled after geese, the distance flown by a pinkfoot from the highlands of Iceland to Norfolk. Barnacle geese gather at Holkham Lake prior to breeding.

Monday 1st February

I saw not geese today, but a hare. It was crouched at the edge of a field, at the seam where a wildlife headland met a crop of oilseed rape. I had inched my bike along almost two miles of a nowhere lane – thick with mud from harvested sugar beet – until I found the same metre of hedgerow in a photo that a friend had sent.

Further back along the lane I'd seen two shelduck at a flooded hollow in a field. At the earliest hint of spring they spread out in pairs across the land, these dashing, chestnut-chested ducks, eschewing their coastal winter flocks. They flew along the lane, above me, bills wax-red in the lunchtime sun, dropping muttered whistles as they went.

I stopped at an ugly right-angled branch, hacked by a clumsy flail. Putting my hand in my pocket to check it

The Meaning of Geese

against the grainy photo on my phone, I saw the hare. A negligible fraction of our Norfolk hares lack all tawny pigment in their fur. Where a typical hare is tan, these precious animals are white; though grizzled flecks still mark their coats, rendering them silver. Beside me, eleven years since I saw one last, was a silver hare.

I had heard about this exquisite animal by chance. My friend knew nothing of our silver hares and sent his photo asking what it was. It had made his day, he said. Among North Norfolk gamekeepers and farmers, silver hares must always have been known; but these lovely things are almost mythically rare. Few photographs exist; few naturalists can claim to have seen one.

The silver hare lay folded in its form, moon-beautiful, its long ears flat along its back. Checking branch by branch and stump by stump for the hare's distinctive spot, my red bike and I had trespassed close, with just the winter-naked hedge between us. The hare was still for long enough for me to crouch and raise binoculars and wish, for once, I owned a camera; but then it calmly loped along the headland and turned onto a tyre track across the field. Here it sat, stretched up, and let me watch. No other, lesser, hare was near.

Once it had gone, into the lost ground beyond the brow, I started home, a great smile across my face. Nature, I know, is heartless, driven only by the sibling needs to prosper and to reproduce. This hare, though – this silver hare, which let me see it – was nothing less than blessing.

Thursday 4th February

As days grow longer, use of the landscape by our two most numerous grey geese is changing fast. Almost the first birds I

February

saw at home this morning were four greylags, flying upriver. Throughout the day I encountered greylags everywhere I went. They may be weeks from laying eggs, but they are leaving winter flocks and spreading across North Norfolk now, reclaiming sites in which they mean to breed.

Pinkfeet, by contrast, have contracted to the coast. In James McCallum's first book, *Wild Goose Winter*, he charts three phases of their Norfolk sojourn. In the first they feed in coastal grazing marshes and nearby summer stubbles. As soon as sugar beet is lifted, they start to feed in harvested fields. More recently, this has included maize fields too. Towards winter's end, as thousands of pinkfeet leave us, to stage in Lancashire, prior to flying on to Iceland, those which remain withdraw to coastal marshes and feed on grass again. The pinks have largely entered this last stage now.

Skylarks sang along the Dry Road as I pedalled to the coast this morning. I heard a singing yellowhammer too – under his breath, as though unsure he knew quite how – and the day was full of mistle thrushes' half-dreamed, Wagnerian voices. A pheasant gave ballistic double-coughs, a song thrush shrilled, and it was mild.

The new flood between Wells and Holkham was busy with waterfowl: wigeon drakes, heads molten in unwonted sun, and graphite gadwall crowding round dispassionate ducks. Above them marsh harriers displayed, buoyant on the fledgling thermals of the year; beyond, on Quarles Marsh, thousands of pinkfeet grazed.

A solemn jury of herons had gathered around the Iceni fort, a lone great egret with them, each waiting to dagger a careless field vole in the winter-yellowed grass. In front of them Holkham's flock of Russian whitefronts grazed, their orange legs and frosted foreheads visible at great distance in

The Meaning of Geese

the kind spring light. Last week Andy counted 300 of them on the marsh.

The usual band of Egyptian geese was by the Marsh Farm track, halfway to Whincover and Burnham Overy, and with them was a single pinkfoot. I was composing this goose's story in my head – how it came to be alone while thousands of pinks were in the marsh beyond – when two cattle egrets strutted past the horses at the farm, in their ungainly way. I'm still shocked whenever I see cattle egrets in Norfolk – so recently have they settled here – shocked and frightened too by what it means for our warming climate, and all our other wildlife.

I had more immediate worries, though. Lowering my binoculars from the egrets I cycled on, feeling at once that my back wheel needed air. I laid my bike down in the verge to pump the tyre but – air hissing from its somehow-ruined valve – in seconds it was absolutely flat.

By the shortest route, south along the lovely valley of the Burn, I was thirteen miles from home. I began to walk, wheeling my wounded bike beside me, its rhythm sounding on the tarmac as we went: two squeaky quavers and a buzzing crotchet. Larks lit our way. A collared dove sang. Two purring rooks launched into crazy helter-skelters above my head. A common gull – weeks yet from its upland nest – burst into shrieking song.

Reaching home, after cycling fourteen miles and walking thirteen more, my legs were lumpish, my back tyre shredded, and my arms sore from hitching up the saddle to spare the metal wheel; but I was rich in birds. I'd seen two dozen bramblings in a hedge, sporting their pitch-and-amber breeding plumage; heard buzzards low above their nesting woods, and a drumming great spotted woodpecker. In spite of heavy legs,

February

and heavy snow forecast for the next few days, spring had spoken to me, through the birds.

Saturday 6th February

A mystery has been solved today. Not in the field – as it has poured unceasingly with rain since dawn, and my beleaguered bike is in the shop – but on the internet.

On 2nd December – a day of mist, raw rain and a long bike ride – Ash, Nick and I saw a glorious pinkfoot flock on Pound Lane east of Docking. I was shivering against the front flank of their van, when, half hidden by the hedge, I saw a goose with a white blaze and an all-pink bill, which I felt at first must be a Russian whitefront. A moment's examination showed, despite the gloom, a blue-grey back with wide pale bars and the same buff breast as on the pinkfeet all around it. Moments later I lost the goose behind the hedge.

Once the geese had flown, and I could safely move without alarming them, I asked the boys whether they too had seen a pinkfoot with a whitefront's face; but they had not. Later, in the wheat field where we found the geese again, Ash saw an adult whitefront. I assumed that – cold, tired and peering through a rain-smeared scope – I must have been mistaken. I angrily chastised myself as I cycled fifteen drizzly miles to home.

Today a Lancashire birder – Stuart Darbyshire – posted photos on Twitter of the same strange goose I saw in December, and my dear friend Mark Golley replied that he had seen it in Norfolk this winter too: an extraordinary pinkfoot with a white blaze and an all-pink bill.

What I love about this story are its many layers. This goose, hatched on Icelandic tundra – among golden plovers, snow buntings and purple sandpipers – possesses, thanks to misspelled genetic code, two exceptional features, which make it distinctive in the field. Months after I briefly saw the bird – and bullied myself into believing I was mistaken – the subtle miracle of the internet has brought it back to me, confirming it was indeed in Norfolk this midwinter, and that today it is in Lancashire, bound again for Iceland.

Far more remarkable – for at the time Icelandic pinkfeet were ten times less numerous, far less was known of them, and the internet was decades from existing – is the story of Old Pink, which Peter Scott recounts in *Morning Flight*, most lyrical of all his books. Published in 1935, it charts the artist's conversion from wildfowler to wildfowl keeper and conservationist.

Before the war, Scott watched his local Norfolk goose flocks lovingly, and among them he often saw a strikingly pale female bird, which he named Old Pink. 'On her right shoulder was a single dark bar, not very noticeable, but nevertheless plainly visible. She was mated with a rather small gander with a few white feathers on his forehead.'

This was not the last Peter Scott heard of Old Pink and her mate. Astonishingly, the following summer, with a friend, he encountered her on a nest of five eggs on a lava cliff in Iceland, her distinctive gander standing sentinel nearby.

Nor even was this the end of his relationship with the goose. Next winter he saw her near his Norfolk home again and she was recorded once more in Iceland the following summer. Thereafter she was never seen: 'With anxiety we watched the packs of pinkfeet in the autumn, but she never came.'

It is hard, reading this account, not to remember Gallico's *The Snow Goose*, which was published just five years later in

February

1940. For Rhayader too was a gentle loner of the marsh, who stood each autumn by his lighthouse, waiting for his friends the geese to come, hoping that among them would be the lone white goose he loved.

Perhaps next winter my bike and I will once again travel around the muddied lanes of Norfolk, in search of geese. Perhaps among the pinkfeet that we see one will have a white blaze and an all-pink bill. For now, it is in Lancashire, and heading north to Iceland, to the upland tundra, there to breed. I wish it luck; and I wish it safely back.

Sunday 7th February

My great-aunt Deborah, who left me many books, including her yellowed copy of *Morning Flight*, was a friend of wildlife artist J. C. Harrison. Taken, as a child, to her solemn home, I would gaze at the many Harrison watercolours on her walls, and she would tell their stories. One was of a capercaillie which she had found dead on the road through a Scottish pine grove, many years before. She had popped it under the bonnet of her Mini and driven it home for Jack to paint.

My favourite painting was of geese on a grassy marsh, with a cold blue sky, the Cotswolds in the background. Most of the birds were Russian whitefronts. Three barnacles stood to the left, while alone at the front of the flock was an adult red-breasted goose. Peter Scott himself had shown her this wild Slimbridge redbreast in the 1950s, Auntie Deborah said, while she was an officer in the army. In awe, I imagined her in a hide far out on the marsh with my hero, as they watched this gorgeous bird. Jack Harrison later rendered the geese from her description, and I dearly loved his painting. The relative who has it now texted me a photograph today and, seeing it, I was transported to those childhood conversations with my powdered and austere great-aunt.

Two red-breasted geese were seen among Slimbridge's Russian whitefronts in the 1950s: the first over several weeks early in 1954 and the second in 1959. The goose in Auntie Deborah's painting was surely one of these. Perhaps the barnacle geese she saw beside it had also flown from Siberia with the whitefronts. More likely, they had merely wandered from the tame flock kept at Slimbridge, as this behaviour is recorded in the Wildfowl Trust's annual report for 1953–54.

Several red-breasted geese have been recorded here in Norfolk too, including two that I have seen, but when Stevenson published *The Birds of Norfolk* the species sat only very tentatively on the county list. 'The only example' he writes, 'of this beautiful and extremely rare species, recorded as procured in Norfolk, is the one mentioned by most of our local authorities as purchased by the late Mr. Lilly Wigg in the Yarmouth Market. This specimen, however, according to contemporary evidence, was plucked and eaten and its claim to a place in the Norfolk list must rest entirely on the credibility of the statements respecting it.'

BirdLife International is, sadly, entirely credible when it lists the red-breasted goose as globally vulnerable, on account of its small and declining population (of which estimates vary from 40,000 to 60,000 birds). Seventy per cent of its population breeds on the Taymyr Peninsula in Siberia, with the rest on nearby tundra. Up to ninety per cent of red-breasted geese now winter on the Black Sea, in Bulgaria and Romania, where illegal hunting is a significant threat, as it is along the birds' migration through Russia and Ukraine. This lustrous goose also faces twin threats from the petrochemical

February

industry: both disturbance by oil extraction in Siberia, and the looming, by now familiar, peril of climate change, which models suggest will render sixty-seven per cent of breeding habitat inhospitable by 2070. Ironically, wind turbines in the winter range – source of renewable energy though they are – appear to affect the birds' feeding. Many new windfarms have been proposed.

To lose the red-breasted goose would be unpardonable. For it is the finest among geese. Smaller and neater than a brent, its black back and waistcoat are separated by a broad and jagged band of white. Its breast and a lopsided square behind its eye are liver-chestnut, crisply edged in white. A round white spot sits on its black face, between a tiny bill and sparkling eye. A wild red-breasted goose seems always active, plucking rapidly at grass, its black mane raised as it angles down its head to feed.

Sitting on a stool, beneath Jack Harrison's delicate painting, my child self longed to see a wild red-breasted goose. Though forty years have passed, and I have had the joy of seeing red-breasted geese, I ache to see one still.

Tuesday 16th February

Since my tyre valve blew, almost two weeks ago, I have been grounded: not by my bike repairs, but by a cold front which stunned us from the east, pushing hapless woodcock ahead of it. Hundreds of these timid leafmould birds have washed up dead on beaches down the coast.

This heartless weather has kept me off my bike. For four days it snowed, almost without a break. The temperature then dipped still lower, freezing ponds, fingers and roads. Finally, a bitter wind arrived and the snow began to drift.

The Meaning of Geese

I hated it. I walked, of course, crunching in neoprene wellies through deep snow, tiptoeing over sheets of ice on roads. I pitied every bird I saw: parties of long-tailed tits in riverside reed, desperate for every calorie that they could find; snipe and woodcock flitting above hostile marshes glassed with ice; and bands of meadow pipits skating over frozen floods, picking at neglected motes which might be food.

Through a year of lockdowns I've coped with being almost entirely alone. Since July I have managed almost without work, tightening my belt and filling empty time as best I could. All winter I have hurtled after geese by bike – covering 900 miles so far to watch them – just to keep my mind and body moving. These last few icy days – no bike, no geese, and not a new word written – have been bleak.

Yesterday a blessed thaw began, though roads remained too frozen for me to cycle. Today, from dawn, it poured. At lunchtime, finally the rain gave way. I pumped my tyres and cycled downriver to the scrape, past north-facing banks still deeply covered in snow, and crops lying wilted by the week-long freeze. Larks sang though, primed by a temperature rise of more than ten degrees in just two days.

Whenever February snow retreats, spring starts. Change can be achingly slow at first: nights still fiercely cold, and days weighed down by cloud and bitter rain. But longer days and surging hormones soon see blackthorn flowers breaking, butterflies on the wing, and birds defending territory. This afternoon the Wensum scrape was noisy with displaying geese.

Among the many feral Canada geese gathered at the scrape, one pair was in display. I heard them first, bugling lovingly as they swam. The male stretched up his neck, tilting it back, exposing his whitish breast above the water. Beside

February

him, as though signalling she felt protected, the female bathed, plunging herself forward. The gander joined her, both birds splashing happily, until another Canada goose swam by. The pair reached their black necks forward along the water, threatening the interloper.

These elegant Canada geese were not the only birds with breeding on their minds today. Above me, from the ragged crown of a centennial oak, a starling clicked and whirred, until a pair of jackdaws knocked him – literally – off his perch. House sparrows chattered in the blackthorn next to me, and, from the scrape beyond, a water rail gave his belching shriek. A blackbird, quickened by the thaw, began to mutter half-remembered phrases from last year's song; and in his lovely voice the winter died.

Many greylags were in the cattle pasture on the valley side, most of the flock unseen beyond the brow of what in Norfolk passes for a hill. Just once the birds came forward, half into view. Among the several hundred greylags here, their wedge bills shining in the cloud-break light, I saw the heads and necks of Norfolk's two roaming snow geese. Will they too stay to breed?

Two more greylags started shouting by the river to my left, seeing off perceived intruders. I watched in fascination, for the offenders were a mismatched pair: the gander a greylag, but the goose a Canada. Such star-crossed matings are not uncommon where both species breed. The territorial pair ran furiously at the greylag gander – their necks out, and orange bills thrust forward, clanging angrily – but they took no notice of his Canada mate, even when they stood just inches from her. Her long black neck and bill, her mid-brown back, her bold white cheek failing altogether to elicit a stereotypical response.

A redpoll flew by, calling somewhere in the clouds. A peregrine – dagger sharp – slammed past, stirring the gulls. I stood leaning on the gate, thinking about geese. All winter these feral birds have stayed together in their flocks, for safety. Now the tug of territoriality grows stronger, spring's hormones more acute. The threads which held their winter flocks together have begun to fray, as breeding looms.

Wednesday 17th February

Most of Norfolk's winter pinkfeet have gone north. Those that remain have largely retreated to coastal grazing marshes, where they both feed and roost. There is little chance that this winter they will suffer the harrowing effects of fog. It happens, every few years, that thick fog moves in from the sea in daylight, while pinkfeet are feeding on inland fields. When evening comes, and geese try to reach the safety of their coastal roosts, they swiftly become disoriented. Flocks can spend the whole night – panicked and exhausted – flying through the fog. On such nights, birders across North Norfolk hear their distressed, insistent voices low above their houses.

James describes these fog events in *Wild Goose Winter*, mentioning in particular the 13th November 1995, when birds called above North Norfolk through the night. But such events are far from new. The oddest on record – resulting in a pinkfoot being arrested – is recounted by the Rev. H. T. Frere, in Henry Stevenson's *The Birds of Norfolk*. On a foggy night in the mid-1800s, a flock of pinkfeet was attracted to the town of Diss, apparently by streetlights. It being Sunday evening, the people were in church, where the voices of the geese above the roof disturbed the service. The panicked

February

birds kept up their clamour from seven in the evening until two in the morning when the fog retreated.

'One bird,' Frere says, 'happened to fly so low as to strike a gas lamp outside the town just as a police constable was passing by, who very properly, as the bird was making a great noise outside a public house, took it into custody, and the next day, being quite unhurt, it was sent off to Dr. Kirkman's lunatic asylum, at Melton, where it lived for some years, and may possibly be alive now. It proved to be a rather small specimen of the pink-footed goose.'

I was not lost in fog as I cycled north today, but my vision was handicapped. Two weeks ago, when my tyre valve blew near Burnham Overy, I somehow also lost the shades I wear to shield my eyes from wind and spray. Each time a lorry shuddered by this morning, I squeezed my eyes tight shut, to keep them safe from salt and grit. All the same, my eyes were angry by the time I reached the coast.

The marsh felt empty as I freewheeled down from Wells. For five months, every time I've come to Holkham, pinkfeet have yapped in lazy lines over the National Nature Reserve or flown inland above my head to feed on beet. On Quarles Marsh I could see a distant group today – a few hundred birds at most – but the sky was silent, save for a greenfinch wheezing in the village. Creature, as I am, of spring, and sun, and birdsong, I was surprised the pinks' departure weighed so heavily. All winter they have been my flock and the day seemed sorrowful without them.

Not all the geese had left, though. I cycled the length of Lady Anne's Drive, where wigeon, teal and shoveler crowded on the floods and battered grass; and lapwings launched themselves in tentative display. Halfway along, I heard a note which made me squeeze my brakes and scan. Westward, the

The Meaning of Geese

sky was loud with pinkfeet: two thousand – maybe more – had flown up from the marsh. They circled, yelling, until whatever danger they perceived had passed.

I chained my bike, to walk along the south fringe of the pines, lured by the siren gossip of pinkfeet in the grazing marsh. Creeping through the oak woods by the sandy track, I reached the low earth bank, built when the tide was banished and the marshes claimed for humans. I knelt, cold water – last week's snow – sucked by my trouser legs to grasp my knees, and raised my head an inch above the bank. I smiled. Even after all these miles and all these months I lose myself in geese.

These pinkfeet were relaxed. A few were grazing; most just standing still, or milling. At the far end of the flock, towards Burnham Overy, a single barnacle plucked at grass, tiny beside the pinks. The day was grey, and, after twelve miles' cycling, and many minutes' crouching, I soon grew cold. I walked to Salts Hole where – beyond two buffy pairs of little grebes and a female goldeneye, diving through the murky water after food – the flock stretched out across the grazing marsh. Salts Hole: I saw my first four pinkfeet of the season here in September.

Further along the track, the tortured claws of bracken lay flattened by the snow, their colour answered in a kite's tail low overhead. Chartreuse lichens encrusted spindly elms and downy reed heads reached for the gloomy sky. Around the fort, a dozen whitefronts grazed.

The next white-fronted geese I saw – some seventy – were further south, seen from the north wall of the park, close to the keeper's pen of Pekin bantams. Stopping to watch them, I leaned my bike against the old brick wall and laughed aloud. For here, beside my new back tyre, my missing shades lay on

February

the grass: wet and muddy, newly emerged from under snow, but found. I rinsed them with the water from my bottle, dried them on my t-shirt, put them on, and cycled – eyes again protected – to Whincover and Burnham Thorpe, and Egmere, Barsham and the Wensum.

Here, by the river, right behind my home, I saw a pair of greylags on the bank: the first of our local pairs back on territory this spring.

Tuesday 23rd February

There is a brute south wind this week and cycling back from the coast today was punishing. All the same, two miles from home, my legs spent from battling against the blow, my bike and I together crossed a threshold: a thousand miles since, in September, we started cycling after geese.

If you draw a line on Google Earth from the North Norfolk coast to Iceland's central highlands, it measures a thousand miles. It has taken me a winter – until the sunny February day on which I've seen my first drone fly of 2021, on which wooded banks are bright at last with waxy snowdrops – to cycle a pink-footed goose's southward autumn migration, which the bird can complete in just a day. These thousand miles do not include the geese's daily feeding flights inland, their regular movements from North Norfolk to the Broads, their wider journeys in hard weather or if food is scarce, nor of course their northbound flight in spring. My pedalling is trivial beside the pilgrimage of our Arctic geese; but it is my homage to them, and my puny protest for their melting tundra.

On Saturday afternoon, after watching brents and whitefronts in the marshes, I cycled home through Holkham Park and counted seventy-four barnacle geese at their breeding site by the lake. I texted Andy who responded with surprise, for in the morning he had seen just fourteen. Nobody yet knows where these barnacles go when they abruptly leave Holkham in August, but Andy and I have witnessed them beginning to arrive.

Barnacles are Arctic geese, which time their egg-laying so their chicks hatch in midsummer. Beneath the midnight sun, the tundra attains its heady peak of energy and life, and goslings have the greatest chance of growing fast and fat, ahead of their first migration and first winter in a European marsh. But Holkham's birds – whatever their origin may be – are fast adapting to life at temperate latitudes. From eggs laid early in the spring, their first chicks may hatch before the end of April, in time with feral Canadas and greylags. Thus, unlike Norfolk's winter pinkfeet, which will stage for another month in Lancashire before leaving us for Iceland; unlike our dark-bellied brents, which will dawdle up Europe's northwest shoulder all through May; unlike Svalbard's migratory barnacle geese, which may yet spend several weeks along the Solway; Holkham's barnacles are reaching their breeding site already.

I could see just two pairs of Holkham's barnacles when I reached the lake this morning. One pair was in the water, bathing. The female dunked her head repeatedly, bright beads of sunlit water splashing from her short black bill and tumbling down her velvet neck to join the lake again. Almost every time she ducked, her stout-necked gander followed suit. For minutes on end the birds were lost in their watery, ritual dance.

Hearing the scratchy yap of geese behind me, I turned to scan. At the far edge of the cricket pitch, half-hidden by three tall oaks, some forty more barnacles were grazing. I tiptoed closer – freezing every time they raised their heads – sat on a bench, and through my scope I joined their flock.

If you look for two hours at forty late-winter barnacle geese, you see they are both immaculately beautiful and hugely varied. Where the black silk stocking of each bird's neck abruptly meets the pearl grey of its belly and flanks, a finger of grey reaches up by the bend of each wing. These fingers look as though they long to meet behind the goose's neck; but they are thwarted by the solid square of black between its shoulders. On each goose this pattern is minutely different.

Each goose's face is distinctive too. Some faces in the flock are white; others faintly yellowish; still others almost apricot. Where the neck's black stretches onto each goose's crown, the pattern also differs: some have a neat black skullcap, squared above the eyes; some have a cowlick, jutting forwards. The black feathers between the bill and eyes are varied too: some geese have a neatly pencilled line, while others sport a sixties singer's brooding smudge. On some birds a small black streak continues behind each eye, towards the corners of the cap.

I saw patterns of goose behaviour by the lakeside too. While the greylag geese around them largely slept, most of the barnacles were feeding, their lustrous necks right-angled downwards, stout bills pulling rapidly at blades of grass, several tugs per second. Whenever a goose dozed off, its eye was briefly sealed by a whitish nictitating membrane. One goose once yawned, revealing its bold pink tongue, in contrast with the elegant monochrome of its plumage.

From time to time a pair of geese, sometimes trailing last year's young, would leave the group, flying to the far side of the lake. First the gander of the pair would raise his neck

The Meaning of Geese

and start to twitch his head. Next he gave a rasping bark, encouraging his mate to follow him. Together the pair then flew, calling loudly as they went. I listened attentively, hoping to detect a difference between male and female calls; but here too each goose was different. In some pairs one bird had a high-pitched yelp, the other deeper. In others both geese sounded the same to me. I scratched my head and resolved to listen to more barnacles.

In half an hour the whole flock was on the far side of the lake, still shouting. Males reached forward with their necks, admonishing families which had strayed too near. Sometimes, in rage they hurtled at offending birds, kinking their necks back in a Z on braking. I texted Andy later, with news of what I had seen. 'Did they do that waddling charge, like fat torpedos?' he replied. Exactly that. We texted back and forth, pondering the origin of Holkham's barnacles; sharing notes and questions on behaviour; looking forward to ringing some of them with Kane this summer, once the geese have bred and moulted.

Summer. Even with the snow gone and the wind now in the south, with flowers breaking into bloom along the sheltered south wall of the park – blue field speedwell, common chickweed, red dead-nettle and hairy bittercress – even with nuthatches and treecreepers singing in the woods around me, the world is whipped and cowering still, and summer seems remote.

Saturday 27th February

Just as the geese are now pulled from their winter flocks by the urge to breed, I am pulled from geese by the flowers, the insects and the birds of spring. These past two days the

February

weather has been wonderful: spring skies and sun, troubled only by a chill north wind and, here and there, a cotton cloud.

Wildlife has responded. Working yesterday at my desk I heard the papery panic of a butterfly against the window in the room behind me. I got up to free a small tortoiseshell, my first of 2021. Later I saw two buff-tailed bumblebee queens – blundering in their fresh-from-hibernation way – and propped my bike against the verge to photograph a clump of primroses with my phone. After the long and ghettoised winter we've endured, these little lives are redolent with meaning.

Today I cycled to the village of my childhood. A friend saw a goshawk here this week, above the dark plantation where I used to watch red deer and follow barn owls down the rides. If ever a day was made for watching goshawks, it was today. I stayed at home until after nine, waiting for the blessed sun to warm the morning, sending the hawks aloft.

As soon as I reached the familiar concrete pad, from which a mile of woodland can be seen, I started seeing buzzards, riding the day's first thermals. I stood two hours there, eyes smarting in the wind and unaccustomed sun, and always there were buzzards. Sparrowhawks joined them in display, and distant kites. Behind me – two weeks earlier than I would ever have expected as a child – a chiffchaff sprang into his syncopated song. Despite the climate fears such changes strike in me, I smiled to hear this old friend's simple voice.

A goshawk has a presence unlike any other bird's. Learning to identify distant raptors by the way they cross the sky, a beginner birder interrogates a thousand sparrowhawks, willing every one to be a goshawk. But when at last you see a goshawk – see its deep and powerful flap; the bulging secondary feathers of its wings; its broad-based, round-tipped tail; its fateful arrow head – there is no doubt.

The Meaning of Geese

I saw three goshawks above the brooding canopy of spruce and pine today. The first two – males – briefly appeared above the woods together, rolling in their buoyant way. The third – a female – plunged chest-first into a roller-coaster dive, an innocent white puff of feathers wrapping around her lethal hips. Each goshawk is as thrilling as your very first.

Skylarks sang, of course – it's early spring in Norfolk and there are always larks – rooks cawed and gurgled, and a pair of greylags flew to a pond where I've known them since it was dug. Their calls admonished me, as they went, for wasting time on hawks.

MARCH

decisions with unintended consequences

As the last pinkfeet leave, and spring wildlife replaces them, I ponder their future in our farming landscape. A friend in Lancashire shares his lifelong love of pinkfeet, while they stage on the Ribble bound for Iceland. Brent geese return to coastal saltmarsh, prior to their journey to Siberia.

Wednesday 3rd March

Before my winter with geese is altogether done, I have some questions still to ask.

In November, I saw our great goose flocks driven relentlessly from the beet and maize fields in which they needed to feed. Seeing them shot at, fleeing in noisy, panicked waves, was harrowing. James and Andy, in particular, are worried for the future of Norfolk's pinkfeet. They believe they'll leave us altogether – no longer come each winter – if they are not afforded space to feed. The management of North Norfolk farms is critical for our geese, as for almost all our wildlife; so today I went to speak to Andy's manager, Jake Fiennes,

The Meaning of Geese

Holkham's director of conservation, who has ambitious plans for biodiversity on the estate, including geese.

The cold was bitter as I cycled north along the Dry Road, the land lost beneath a spiteful fret. At Barsham the tic-tac orange bills of oystercatchers pierced the gloom; and, despite the cold, a hundred unseen larks entwined my way with song. I found Jake at the north end of Lady Anne's Drive, from where we walked together through the Gap onto the beach. Before we took a hundred steps our conversation bounded across half a dozen subjects. 'I digress,' said Jake, fixing me in his flax-blue gaze. 'I'm a bastard for that.'

Jake has trodden a non-conformist path to reach the position of respect he holds in conservation; but he's the more effective for it. Were he a bird, this tall, lean man would be an Arctic skua. Skua-like, his wild mind twists and banks, from one theme to another, but all the while his steely focus is on delivering a better landscape for our wildlife: just as a skua's attention on a sandeel in a tern's bill is unrelenting. Watching autumn skuas in Norfolk, as they harry hapless Sandwich terns for food, I sense that they enjoy their piracy. Jake too, enjoys the game he plays; in which wildlife is the winner.

'This is where the dogs-on-leads zone begins,' he said, as blown sand whipped our ankles. Last summer, all along the Norfolk coast, ground-nesting birds were flushed from nests and even killed by dogs, as people spilled across the landscape, gasping for freedom after locked-down months. It was a grim time for reserve wardens. In response, Jake and his team have taken action, with Natural England, to protect the ringed plovers and little terns which nest on Holkham beach. 'I was asked to help fund a report on dog impacts along the coast,' Jake told me. 'I said no. I already know there are impacts, so I'm doing something about it. I may not get it right first time, but I'm doing something.' Following public consultation, he and the team have zoned the beach. This year they'll gauge how visitors and their dogs respond, and whether zoning translates into better productivity for vulnerable beach-nesting birds.

This active, practical approach to conservation informs everything Jake does. His career began in South Norfolk, on Sir Nicholas Bacon's Raveningham Estate, which he joined as a junior gamekeeper. Having grown up scrabbling through bushes after animals, finding fascination in their lives, Jake loathed the poisoned sterility he found in modern agriculture, in which the landscape had been stripped of hedges, meadows, ponds, soil health and living things. Unafraid of conflict, he questioned everything he saw. In time he was put in charge. The regenerative farming methods he introduced, and the wildlife which came flooding back, attracted attention far beyond South Norfolk. After twenty-four years at Raveningham, Jake moved to Holkham, charged with managing the National Nature Reserve and reversing declines in wildlife right across the estate.

We spoke of geese, of course, as we strode at Jake-speed across the chilly beach. I raised the problem of farmers drilling wheat as soon as sugar beet is harvested; then driving goose flocks off the crop. 'Decisions with unintended consequences,' Jake answered bluntly, his breath scented by a roll-up cigarette. 'With better harvesters, the farmers made a deal to sell the sugar beet tops to British Sugar. They used to be discarded and left in the fields for geese. They now plant cereals straight away after harvest because the soil is drier. The beet has sucked the water out, and it's better for cultivation. Plus the soil is wrecked, and they know it. They plant quickly to heal it, to hold it down.

The Meaning of Geese

They then don't like it when the geese come, because their feet cap the top layer of the soil; so they drive them off. They've created their own conflict.'

I asked what could be done to fix it. 'We need a sacrificial crop we can feed the geese in,' Jake answered, his mind racing with excitement. 'If you have the geese, everything else will come. The ideal is carbon capture combined with biodiversity net gain, across every farm.' He broke off, the better to emphasise his crucial point: 'But I want the farmers to find the solutions. I want them to get the credit. We know the issues – climate, agricultural policy, economics – but there's an opportunity for us all to do so much better.'

'The average farmer is 67, and used to getting handouts, but the outlook and attitudes of young farmers are so different. When I talk to young farmers their minds are wide open. They talk in terms of soil healing and biodiversity benefit. I believe there is real hope; an opportunity for farmers to be the solution.'

I remarked how rare it was to meet an optimist in conservation. 'I spoke to a farmer recently,' Jake replied, 'who had planted buckthorn in his hedge. He was thrilled because he'd seen his first brimstone in forty years, as a result. This sort of thing is possible. You've got to work with farmers,' he insisted, conviction audible in his voice. 'They manage seventy-five per cent of the landscape, so it's the biggest win.'

Jake is ambitious for our wildlife, driven to reverse the appalling losses suffered across the landscape in the twentieth century. 'I've only been here two breeding seasons. Last year the lapwing population was up by fifty per cent and their productivity up 100 per cent.'

Our conversation bounded on, from books to matted sea-lavender and the spread of Chinese water deer across

East Anglia. 'I shot my first,' he said, flashing me a skua's smile. 'In the tradition of the old naturalists, I wanted to be sure I'd seen one.'

We crossed the muddy saltmarsh which has formed in Holkham Bay, setting linnets clattering from last year's tired sea purslane. Reaching the north of Lady Anne's Drive, I thanked Jake for his thoughts on geese and landscape. 'Always a pleasure, Nick,' he said. 'Thanks for getting me out of the bloody office.' With this he strode off to his truck, lighting a cigarette, in preparation for another Zoom call with Natural England.

Tuesday 16th March

With the pinkfeet gone, and brents and whitefronts leaving soon, this is the point at which a decent author would head northward with their flocks. After a spell in Lancashire, where Norfolk's winter pinks are largely staging now, I would migrate to Iceland in the spring, stopping first in southern meadows with the geese; continuing as they moved to upland tundra in early summer. Finally – as our tale of geese crescendoed to its peak – I would reach some mosquito-maddened Siberian peninsula for midsummer, there to watch dark-bellied brent geese and Russian whitefronts nesting beneath the deathly wings of gyrfalcons, and the undying sun.

But I have not cycled a thousand lonely miles and more, only to climb aboard a plane to make a more compelling dénouement. Nor, I have realised as I've learned all winter from friends and colleagues, are the geese's lives in Iceland and Siberia mine to tell. At every point along their journeys, our winter geese have different meanings in the landscape

The Meaning of Geese

and in people's lives; meanings beyond my understanding. How facile it would be for me to write about them in places which I barely know, when everywhere that Norfolk's geese migrate to breed people have spent lifetimes studying them.

Instead of flying, I shall travel with the geese in my imagination, and try to tell their story in the words of those who know the northern landscapes they frequent, and love them. The first of these goose witnesses is Stuart Darbyshire. One of Lancashire's most expert goose-watchers, Stuart is a friend of many of our Norfolk watchers too. The time we shared on Zoom today sped by, with Stuart freely sharing years of knowledge and commitment, laced with his understated northern wit.

'I'm from Lancashire originally,' he said, though his vowels made no such comment necessary, 'from north of the river, in the Fylde. I'm south of the river now, what's called the Inner Ribble. I can't quite see the marshes from my house, but they're close.'

Stuart's goose-watching year is very different from ours in Norfolk. While our pinkfeet arrive from early September and – though roving widely – largely stay until the year is out, on the Ribble Stuart sees two arrivals every year. The first, like ours, comes from the north in early autumn. 'When the geese arrive,' he said, 'they land into the Ribble. What seems to happen is there's an influx in September, which lasts around a month. Then there's a lull here. Many of the geese go north into the Fylde. Quite a lot go down to you.

'Mostly they feed on saltmarsh here.' I cut him off to ask if Lancashire saltmarsh was still grazed; as ours, ungrazed for centuries now, is never used by pinkfeet. 'The vast majority is some degree of grazed land,' he replied. 'Banks Marsh, where I often watch, is cattle grazed, in summer.

March

'The exception is potato fields. It's really good growing soil round here. You get the best views of them in potato fields.' The crack of Norfolk guns still sounding in my mind, I asked how farmers in Lancashire viewed the geese. 'I get more positive reactions than negative among the farmers I speak to,' Stuart said. 'The majority of farmers love having them there. They associate having swans and geese with a high yield the following year because swan crap is so rich. One field which couldn't be harvested was deliberately left for geese and swans this winter – that farmer's great – and it had 1,000 whoopers. That's a lot of crap.'

In a normal year, by mid-October, Stuart's local pinks have dwindled to a thousand birds seen distantly on the saltmarsh, but last autumn was phenomenal. 'I had a week off in October, without family, because a holiday got cancelled thanks to Covid. I wasn't intending to watch geese, but it was just so good.' A boyish grin broke across his darkly stubbled face as he remembered. 'There was this one potato field. I called it the field that kept on giving. Every day there would be a different scarce goose. It was really dark soil that had just been turned over, so the orange legs of the rarer geese just shone. The weather was horrendous though,' he chuckled. 'I was birding under an umbrella. I saw the same dog walker every day, who told me I was crazy.'

Generally, the best of Stuart's goose-watching starts in January. 'We get mega-excited in midwinter when you guys post on Twitter about your flocks, as we just know the good stuff is coming to us. Our pinks pick up from early January, as they come up to us from you, and the rare geese come with them. Three or four years ago we had that redbreast that had been with you, with a big influx of Russian whitefronts.' Again I interrupted, to show him James's painting on my

The Meaning of Geese

wall of that same lost redbreast and the Todd's Canada goose with it, in a flock of pinkfeet. 'We've had two Todd's this year,' he said, 'one in autumn – the bird that came to you – and another distinctive bird just recently, which has come to Lancashire for its third year.

'At the moment the pinks are scattered across the Ribble and the Fylde,' he said. 'There are geese everywhere in Lancashire at the minute. But in April they'll gather at Marshside RSPB reserve, on the south side of the Ribble. There's a time when it feels like all the grey geese in the country are here. Normally we don't see them like you do – they're always far away on the saltmarsh – but when they're due to go they become more accepting. It's like a carpet of geese. We hope for a north wind in April,' he laughed, 'to keep them here. The moment there's a good wind they're off.'

Seeing enthusiasm light his face, I asked Stuart what geese meant to him. His reply, at first, was matter-of-fact. 'Geese are a major part of my birding year, I guess. Lancashire is not a hotspot for rare birds, but where we might not have the quality we have quantity. Wildfowl are the main element of that.' Then emotion crept into his voice. 'The first time you hear the call in autumn, it's magic. Other people can't understand spending the whole day just looking at one flock, but there's nothing so relaxing as working through a flock of geese for something rare. I'm really good at Where's Wally,' he quipped.

Still musing on rare geese, Stuart brought up the grey-bellied brant, which for four years came to Norfolk. One spring he found it on the Ribble, as it headed north from Norfolk with the pinks. He thought at first he must be seeing a black brant from the Pacific, but James – with whom he has struck a friendship, through their common love of geese – helped solve the mystery.

March

'What I like about the goose community is reaching out,' Stuart said. 'You can see someone's photo online and start chatting as though you've known each other for years. There's an energy that passes with the geese. You see the same individual birds in different places and know that other people have seen them, or ringed them.' His mind went northwards with them for a moment. 'I'd love to go to Iceland and see them breeding. And not just there: I'd love to see the breeding grounds of these grey-bellied brants.'

We could have talked for hours, the pair of us fired up with fascination, but Stuart was needed back at work. I thanked him for sharing so much knowledge and his passion for the geese. His eyes smiled cheekily as he replied: 'Goose obsessives, we tend to be alright.'

Wednesday 17th March

On Friday Andy texted with news of a curious group of hybrid geese that had unexpectedly appeared at Holkham: twenty-nine of them, each different but all with features both of cackling and of barnacle geese. The weather has been dreadful ever since – strong wind and unremitting rain – and I've not made it to the coast to see them. When Andy told me, a few days later, that the geese had flown off east, I thought that I had missed these misfits altogether. But the next day they reappeared, in fields north of the church gate to Holkham park: the very fields where, many years ago, I saw my only British cackling goose, in a flock of pinkfeet.

When I was young, endlessly thumbing the pages of Peter Scott's *A Coloured Key to the Wildfowl of the World*, cackling geese and Canada geese were considered all one species, with eleven regional subspecies together covering practically

The Meaning of Geese

the whole of North America. Superficially, all eleven are similar – with brown bodies, black tails, white rumps, black necks, white cheeks, and black legs and bills – but they are hugely varied in size, structure and voice. In 2004 the American Ornithologists' Union concluded that the seven larger-bodied, longer-necked subspecies, which largely breed in temperate regions, formed the Canada goose, while the four small, short-necked tundra-breeding subspecies composed the cackling goose. These charming cacklers look, for all the world, like cartoon Canada geese; though genetically they are closer to Europe's Arctic-breeding barnacle geese than to North America's Canadas.

Today was forecast to be dry and fairly calm – the first such day since Holkham's hybrid flock arrived last week – so I cycled off in hopes of seeing them. After two long, miserable weeks – trapped in my house and head – riding my old red bike again was joy. Close to home I heard a trilling greenfinch, chipper despite the cold, and hawthorn hedges all along my way were blushing green. No colour is more redolent with hope.

Soon, though, the moody bank of cloud above the sea moved south to meet me. By the time I reached the marshes west of Wells the morning's damp and chilly air was manifesting rain. Rain which had not been forecast. I pushed on through the squall – encouraged by the breathy lunacy of lapwings in display – but the rain grew heavier and a cutting wind picked up. This was not to be an easy day for watching geese.

All the same, north of the keepers' houses, I stopped to scan the marsh. There were Russian whitefronts here, greylags, Canadas, Egyptians and a lonely pair of brents, but my attention was quickly stolen by a raven's throaty double-bark. Hounded from lowland England's skies by nineteenth-century gamekeepers and farmers, these splendid birds have only very recently returned to Norfolk. This one was just above me, so close that I could see its jagged beard, its knowing obsidian eye. Every Norfolk raven is still a thrill, even under bitter rain.

As I reached the grassy fields north of the church, the rain came yet more heavily, the wind more keen. Raising rain-blotched binoculars, I took in many greylags, behind which was a group of small, dark geese. Too brown for barnacles, each different, as is typical of hybrids, here was Andy's flock. My plan was to take a portrait of each goose – using my scope as a zoom lens for my phone – to study them and ponder whether any were pure cackling geese. But the rain fell harder still, drenching scope, binoculars and me. For the second time this winter I darkly muttered the name of Tomasz Schafernaker, who four hours ago had promised that the weather would be grey and cold but dry.

I wheeled my bike under the holm oaks beside the field and sat down on an old tree's root, among yellowish, untidy clumps of wood false brome. Somewhat sheltered from the rain, I watched the hybrids closely. Most were clearly intermediate between cackling geese and barnacles: too grey for cacklers, with white foreheads or eyebrows, where a cackling goose has little business being white. One bird was patterned exactly like a barnacle: white-faced with just a line of black connecting its bill, its eye and cap. It had the subtly patterned mantle of a barnacle, each feather pale-based, with a smudgy, dark subterminal bar, fringed even paler at the tip. But instead of the black and powder grey of a pure barnacle goose's back, this bird's mantle was muddied brown. Like a barnacle, but not one. Another among these greyer birds was shaped and patterned exactly like a cackling goose – short neck, steep forehead, stubby bill – but its back was grey, its genes likewise confused.

A small number in the flock were brown, the warm peaty colour of the lesser cackling goose: tiniest subspecies and commonest in captivity. All but one of these had a white wedge on its forehead, betraying barnacle genes. Even the one bird which was shaped and largely coloured like a cackling goose, seemed to have a breast too dark and purplish, echoing the black bib of a barnacle. All, I felt, were hybrids. As Andy wondered when he found the flock, where had so many, so distinctive hybrid birds appeared from? We suspect the Netherlands or Belgium, where keeping exotic waterfowl is commonplace, but we will likely never know.

By now, despite my layers of winter clothes, I was shuddering with cold, my hands raw from the water seeping through my gloves. The geese walked further down the field, beyond the hulking flock of greylags. Turning north into the driving rain, they started bathing in a puddle. I dried my saddle with my sleeve, stowed my sodden telescope and tripod. Then, shivering, I turned for home.

At Barsham, just over halfway back, the sky was speedwell blue; the sun so warm I shed my coat and outer fleece and rolled up my sleeves. Strange weather and strange birds today, but, after two bleak weeks, I'm on my bicycle and watching geese.

Monday 22nd March

The wild world is never at a standstill. Even as the cogs of winter grind down to the solstice, wild lives are always on the move and the season slowly changing. Some days, however, feel more significant. Like mudslips, fires and beaver

March

dams, they quickly change the course of things. Today was such a day.

Even as I left my house, the spring sun warmed my back. Two pairs of greylags flew downriver, calling conversationally, as they do in spring. A chiffchaff sang. The pinkish blossom of a cherry plum softened the sharp blue sky.

At Barsham a pair of lesser black-backed gulls sat in a field of winter wheat. Is anything more handsome than lesser black-backs in spring sunshine, newly here from southern Europe? I love the tapered elegance of their shape, the contrast between their egg-yolk bills and lead-dark backs. They are magnificent, and these the first I've seen this year.

North of Egmere, all the verges were a Champagne froth of flowering alexanders, marked here and there by deadnettles, the red of Beaujolais. The horse-grazed paddocks south of Wells were bright with daises; the year's cogs suddenly turning fast.

The marshes too were thrilling; full of the promise of nests and chicks. West of the town, a Cetti's warbler shouted from a ditch, my first in months. Further on, from far out on the marsh, I heard a chiming band of avocets. Great egrets stood nearby, puffed up above their females hidden in the reed.

As for geese, greylags were everywhere, their flocks disintegrated into pairs, each in a ditch or by a reed-fringed pool, claiming a space for spring. Over the saltmarsh towards Overy I saw a flock of brents, still here for some weeks yet; but pinkfeet, I almost wished I had not seen.

When, on a warm day in September, they arrived, their calls above the pines were rapture. My mind raced forward, to the mud and sugar beet of December, to days spent shivering, lost in flocks of geese; and many such days sustained me through this locked-down winter. But nothing in those goose-loud months prepared me for how hollow the departure of the pinks would feel. Walking out today along the seawall, I smiled to see sweet violet blooms, to hear the reels of skylarks and meadow pipits' insistent songs. Spring is my time. Yet seeing two hundred silent pinkfeet, bunched together on the marsh, was somehow tragic. These were the lost, the failed, the shot, the old, unpaired, unfit for breeding. These were the dregs among the dinning flocks that friends and I have witnessed all this winter long. Beside those turbulent hordes, which filled the bitter winter sky with sound, these few seemed lifeless.

Brooding on their fate, I ambled back along the seawall, under a sharp male peregrine and the horizontal stripes of spoonbills commuting from saltmarsh channels to their colony. Reaching my ruddy-darter-coloured bike I cycled homeward through the park, where yesterday Andy counted 220 barnacle geese, and this morning our roving snow goose pair was seen.

When I arrived, the snow geese were on the cricket pitch north of the hall, in company with fifty greylags. The gander puffed his chest and raised his angular head, guarding his slender female as she grazed. I passed them, to reach my favourite lakeside bench, and counted barnacles: 250 birds, their numbers rising by the day.

Andy texted as I counted: out on the marsh he'd flushed a family of five Russian whitefronts, last of this year's flock. And reading this, I knew my winter with geese was done.

Wednesday 31st March

I cycled into another world today. Since Monday a gentle wind has blessed us from the south, bringing sunshine,

March

Saharan sand and unaccustomed warmth. Today the temperature in North Norfolk reached 24° Celsius.

Nature has responded to this fleeting summer. This morning, all along the Dry Road, copses rang with lilting chiffchaff song. A blackcap muttered from behind a crooked elder, and clumps of lesser celandines turned their happy faces sunwards under every flowering blackthorn hedge. Cycling in just shorts and t-shirt I was hot.

West of Wells the flood felt oddly empty. There were no wigeon; hardly any teal. Just like our geese, the ducks have slipped away, taking their winter voices with them. Their stake in Norfolk's soundspace has been claimed by breeding birds. A redshank gave his joyful rocking song and lapwings tumbled breathily. Although tomorrow's wind will swing back to the north, and temperatures will plummet, this gruelling Covid winter has run its course; and spring has come.

High in the wispy cirrus above the road I heard a Mediterranean gull. My favourite gulls, these scab-billed birds have colonised southern England rapidly of late. This was the first of several of these flawless things I saw and heard today, their sharp yelps a portal to the saltpans in Provence where, aged just twenty, studying for my undergraduate degree, I heard them first.

Peacock butterflies, stirred from hibernation by the sunshine, jousted at one another between the ivied hedges of the track at Whincover. Watching buzzards, kites and harriers over the marsh, I saw, more than a mile away above the pines, stretched necks and silvered wings: a pair of cranes. They drifted west, minding the coast and, in their great-winged shadow, a sedge warbler – the first I've ever heard in March – gave his delirious African song from winter-brittle reed along a ditch.

The Meaning of Geese

Where the seawall meets the dunes I sat for one last time with winter's geese. Brents of course, dark-bellied brents, the saltmarsh geese. Just weeks ago this flock was hundreds strong, and feeding in the grazing marsh. Today I saw just forty-six, drawn back to sad, brown saltmarsh by the first spring flush of eelgrass in the creeks. They too will soon be gone. Sitting in a t-shirt in the sun, the sky above me sobbing with the songs of larks, the wintry burble of the brent geese almost jarred; drawn from a half-forgotten dream.

Before they leave – before these last Siberian geese are gone – I have some questions still to ask, some stories still to hear.

APRIL

the final stanza in this song of geese

I speak to Dafila Scott, Peter's daughter, to understand the work and mind of the great man whose words have travelled with me all winter. Two Icelandic scientists generously share their lives with geese as pinkfeet return to them. My journey with geese comes to its end where it began, at Holkham, as greylag and barnacle goslings hatch beside the lake.

Thursday 1st April

One voice has gone with me all winter, as I've cycled round North Norfolk watching geese: the voice of Peter Scott. He and Gerald Durrell were my heroes as a child. For unlike other celebrated naturalists, it seemed to me, they acted to protect the creatures and wild places they so loved; that I too loved.

It's more than thirty years since Scott's charming paintings taught me all the wildfowl of the world. Ducks, swans and geese bewitched me then, and they have done so ever since. More than any other's, the thoughts and books of Peter Scott have influenced me as I've followed pinkfeet, brents and whitefronts this winter long. In *Morning Flight* Scott speaks for me, and for the many wildfowl-lovers who have helped me: 'There is a peculiar aura that surrounds in my mind anything and everything to do with wild geese. That I am not alone in this strange madness, I am sure;...and I hardly know any that have been able to resist its ravages, when once they have been exposed to infection.'

I wanted to feel close to Peter Scott, to test my imagined understanding of his thoughts and life. Through a mutual friend I wrote to his daughter Dafila – like him an artist and biologist – who warmly agreed to speak to me about him and about her own rich life with geese and swans. Her kindness was doubly meaningful: when I returned to the UK, after a decade spent largely on the southern edge of Amazonia, the first piece of wildlife art I bought was a vivid pastel of Dafila's – of golden plovers and a lapwing sleeping in an orange autumn field – which I loved from the second I saw it.

When we spoke today I asked – what other question could I ask? – what geese had meant in Dafila's life. 'I've had a lucky life,' she said, her eyes bright with the memory, 'in the sense of growing up at Slimbridge. In the early, early days we would sneak up behind the seawall to one of the little hides and watch geese on the Dumbles. We had to be terribly, terribly quiet, as the geese were just on the other side. If you made a noise you got in the most awful trouble.

'And going outside at night was wonderful. Apart from Bewick's swans, there is nothing more beautiful than the sound of white-fronted geese.' She thought a while. 'Of course the nēnēs were pretty important to me too. They were exciting because they were so rare, and they are so very

April

gentle. When you offer them grain they take it so gently. Unlike the greylags.'

Her father's central role in saving the Hawaiian goose, or nēnē, from extinction brought to my mind a question I had long been pondering: having been so passionate about wildfowling, and having written so evocatively of it, was he wistful over giving up? Dafila's response was instant and quietly vehement: 'No, absolutely not. He didn't regret giving up at all. He'd just moved on. He'd become aware of geese as family birds, aware of the awfulness of wounding them. He became more imaginative of what it was like to be an animal.

'He was very much involved in banning whaling. There were two arguments at the time: the impact on their populations and the inhumanity of it. He was concerned by both. On a trip to the Antarctic, he had witnessed the death of a minke whale by harpoon and it took eight minutes. He used to compare this with harpooning a cow in a field. He came to dislike the idea of killing wildlife unnecessarily or for fun. His view was that there was so much more to be gained by watching, studying or photographing it.

'In the same way, he was keen to bring people to see ducks, geese and swans at Slimbridge and the other centres. He wanted people to love things because he understood that if they loved them they would want to conserve them. He felt that wildfowl were fantastic ambassadors for wetland wildlife; both because they're stunningly beautiful and because they're international. There's a mystery about them because of their migrations. Pinkfeet meant an awful lot to him,' she said, reflecting on his lifelong love of geese, 'especially in his early life, but later, at Slimbridge, the whitefronts came to mean a great deal, and the lesser whitefronts too of course.'

The Meaning of Geese

Knowing, from *A Thousand Geese*, that her parents had married on an early pinkfoot expedition, I asked whether Dafila had been to Iceland to watch geese herself. 'No,' she replied, 'I've been to the Russian Arctic and to Alaska, but never Iceland.' Then, with a charming smile, she added, 'There are no Bewick's or whistling swans there. I'm a tundra* swan person, you see.

'When I was young I was unwell. While convalescing at home I got into the Bewick's swan study. My father had realised you could recognise each swan by the pattern on its bill. I became completely hooked. It was such fun; so exciting when they came back the next year and you could see who was with whom and whether they had brought cygnets with them.

'My father had a formula for drawing the swans' bills, from each side and from the front. He insisted on drawing them himself, but finally there were too many swans, and he was too busy with other things, so at last I was allowed to draw the new swans. Later I became a zoologist myself. I did my thesis on Bewick's swans,' she added, with a smile.

'He was a hard taskmaster, my father, and very single-minded. He was driven to make his name separately from his father. When he wanted to do something he did it and everything had to be done right. But he was a very kind man.' I recalled the stories of Scott's kindness that I'd heard over the winter past. 'I'm glad,' said Dafila.

'What would your father be doing now?' I asked. Dafila stopped to think: 'He'd be continuing to make the case for

---

* Bewick's and whistling swans are now considered two forms of a single species, the tundra swan.

April

the natural world. He'd be tackling the crisis on as many fronts as he could. As he grew older he put more and more into conservation. My mother would tell him he had to paint as we needed to eat; but he was always trying to help people love wildlife.'

With Dafila he succeeded, as with millions, including me. A swallow flew past my window as we spoke, the first I've seen in 2021, hope-bearing after the gruelling winter we've endured. 'Swallow,' I blurted, excitement in my voice. And, with the quick, instinctive movement of a bird, Dafila turned to the window by her, hoping she too might see one there.

Friday 23rd April

The final stanza in this song of geese was always to be sung by Icelandic voices; theirs are the pinkfeet now. On the 2nd April – his birthday – Norfolk artist Jonathan Yule heard from Anna, his friend of many years, that the first pinks had reached her farm. He hopes to return this summer to her valley in the eastern uplands, after two years' absence thanks to Covid. All this week the internet has brought me news of geese departing the UK, over the Hebrides, bound for their tundra summer home. At Holkham, winter's mighty flocks of pinkfeet have dwindled now to just five birds, which, Andy tells me sadly, will never leave: too old, too weak, poisoned by lead, pricked by a hunter's pellet.

Icelandic voices have been slow to reach me, though. Each researcher I have spoken to has modestly insisted someone else knows more of geese and could better tell the saga's final tale. I too have been slow to write: lost in the giddy surge of spring, so keenly needed. Grieving the geese's leaving too. They called me on through a long and lonely winter.

Today our resident geese reminded me I owed them a last stanza in their song. At dawn I cycled thirteen miles to a friend's garden in northwest Norfolk; the scrubby common by my house loud as I left with the liquid lisp of willow warblers. Their voices, and those of many others newly here from Africa, have filled the silence left by winter's wigeon, teal and geese.

We sat in my friend's garden drinking coffee, as tree sparrows – cocoa crowned – flew by a dozen times, carrying pigeon feathers to their nest. Tree sparrows are not the rarest birds which breed beside his house. Just fifty yards along a flinty lane, past a rampant clump of creeping comfrey, quick with hairy-footed flower-bees, a woman was picking horse muck from a paddock. 'There he is,' my friend said. To my astonishment, almost beside the woman was a stone curlew, his long legs primrose in the early light. 'The nest is just beyond the fence,' he said, 'behind the tenth post from the corner.' As if in confirmation, the female bird flew up, and landed further down the field. The male, apparently unworried by his human company, hopped across the paddock fence to join his mate; then crept to take his turn brooding their pepper-speckled eggs.

We walked on down the lane, to the territories of two more pairs of stone curlews, and two lapwing pairs, their mottled chicks already hatched. The day warmed quickly; so too the spring around us. Holly blues skipped along the hedge: the day's clear sky distilled into the wings of butterflies. An ashy mining-bee landed on the dusty track, seeking a place to excavate her nest.

April

It was a day of sun – despite the cold wind from the north – of nests and flowers and insects. A day when winter's clamouring flocks of geese seemed fanciful. But leaving the village I passed the pond, where mallard ducklings twirled around their dappled mothers and greylag goslings grazed between their parents' pinkish legs, reminding me I owed it to our winter pinks to see them home to Iceland.

The first Icelandic scientist who agreed to speak to me was Hálfdán Helgi Helgason. A broad young man, round-faced, with tawny beard and ice blue eyes, he is the Icelander of popular imagination. Like all Norse heroes, he's swashbuckling too. Thanking him for joining me, I asked how long he had. 'I have time,' he answered. 'I am not flying, for a reindeer census, until this afternoon.'

Speaking no Icelandic, I asked about his name. 'It means half Danish. I was named after my grandfather, but the name goes quite far back. It's not a compliment,' he added with a chuckle.

True to his name, Hálfdán has lived a half-Scandinavian life. Until the summer of 2019, when he took his job at the East Iceland Nature Research Centre, he had spent ten years in northern Norway. 'I did my MSc on Icelandic puffin survival from long-term ringing data. Then I worked for the Norwegian Polar Institute, coordinating a project tracking eleven seabird species across the North Atlantic with geolocators. You can't study seabirds without looking at the whole system.' I told him of my own voyages to Svalbard, Norway's Arctic archipelago. His voice cracked as he reflected on a decade's work there. 'It's fantastic,' he murmured, almost to himself.

'Now I work with reindeer and with geese, but I'm not a goose specialist.' Each Icelander I have contacted has claimed not to be an expert; has encouraged me to speak to someone else who knows geese better. But Hálfdán does know geese, and more importantly he loves them. 'I started in ornithology in Iceland aged eleven, in 1997 or 1998,' he said. 'I was invited to be a runner for the Wildfowl and Wetlands Trust, catching pinkfeet. I loved it, so I stayed for three or four summers.'

He laughed, remembering one goose among the thousands he has caught. 'It was the most stubborn pink-footed goose we ever came across while ringing. Driving the jeep along a track, we saw a family of geese and decided to get down. One goose ran up a steep slope and I gave chase. I lost track of time and went over the mountain after it. I was gone for two hours. I just had to get that goose! When I came back I was allowed to choose its neck collar.' He chose the letters API, short for the Icelandic word for monkey, in tribute to the goose's pluck.

With geese now flocking back to Iceland, I asked Hálfdán what they meant to him. 'Geese mean spring. But when I stepped outside this morning I saw a group of snow buntings. It is almost spring here, but not yet.' Enthusiasm suddenly flashed across his face: 'I wish I could take the laptop and show you the field below the other side of the building. It's full of greylag, pinkfeet and whooper swans. Let me just go have a peek.' With that he darted from our conversation, lured by spring's returning waterfowl.

He came back beaming. Since I likely saw some 50,000 individual pinkfeet in the winter – ten per cent of the Iceland and Greenland population of the species – I hazarded that Hálfdán might just have seen a goose I knew myself from Norfolk; a goose which Stuart, perhaps, had seen just days before in Lancashire. The three of us bound together by these thrilling birds.

What did Icelandic farmers make of them, I asked? 'Many farmers dislike the impacts of the geese,' Hálfdán said. 'But in mitigation they're hunted in great numbers in late summer, from 20th August when the season starts, especially greylags.' Lately, as Icelandic greylags are believed – from UK winter counts – to be declining, hunters have been encouraged by the government to turn to pinkfeet.

Hálfdán described in detail how this policy has largely failed. Pinkfeet, which breed in Iceland's uplands, only briefly visit coastal fields in spring and autumn. Outside this time, they must be hunted in the evening, by lying in wait beside the upland ponds on which they roost. Greylags, which can be shot from ditches as they fly to lowland fields at daybreak, are much easier to take, and are more popular.

Something made me ask if this handsome outdoorsman was a hunter too. 'I am,' he answered. Then he paused. 'I will be frank with you: I enjoy hunting immensely, but I have very mixed feelings, I love birding. But hunting absolutely takes hold of you.'

I wondered whether hunting was a part of Iceland's cultural heritage. 'As a young man I would have said yes,' he said, 'but looking back at the history, now I would say no. A lot of what you're taught about tradition is not true. You're told the modern puffin hunt is a tradition, but in truth it goes not much further back than the early twentieth century. The *fleygastong* pole nets which are widely used today were not popular until after the Second World War when bamboo became available. Geese are the same. Hunting is very popular in Iceland now. Of course there was always a harvest of geese, for hundreds of years, but they were driven into stone pens on the tundra during moult. Now,' he chuckled at the symmetry, 'we catch the geese for ringing in pens made of the same bamboo poles.' 'You couldn't pick a less Icelandic plant,' I said.

As here in Norfolk, Iceland's geese have many meanings; meanings which shift with time. Our meeting ending, I thanked Hálfdán for his many insights and our warm, wide-ranging conversation. 'I am not a specialist,' he repeated, earnestly. 'You must speak to Skarphéðinn Þórisson, who knows them better. He will tell you many stories.'

So, two days later, I duly spoke to Skarphéðinn. As his laptop camera came to life I saw a very different face: a slim man, his silver hair closely cropped, his eyes framed by large, round spectacles in royal blue. I asked, apologetically, how to pronounce his name and where it came from. 'From a warrior in the Njáls saga,' he replied. I later looked the story up and found that Skarphéðinn lived in the late thirteenth century. A venerable name.

His modern namesake has worked with geese for many years. 'In 1978,' he told me, 'I was hired to carry out an environmental impact assessment for a hydroelectric project in the eastern highlands. I was watching reindeer, to see what impact the dam would have on them, but also watching birds. The pink-footed goose is the main bird in the highlands, so this was the start of my interest in them.

'I was in the highland reindeer calving grounds in May or June 1979. My colleague Kristinn Skarphéðinsson and I found a moulting flock of non-breeding pink-footed geese on the east side of Snæfell, in an area which since 2008 has been included in Vatnajökull National Park. We counted roughly 1,000 geese. Since then I have counted them every

April

year. I am flying to count the reindeer, so I may as well count the geese. The peak was 1991, when we found 13,100 birds. At the time this was the largest moulting flock of pinkfeet in the world.

'A lot has changed since I started. You have half a million of them in Britain in winter now.' I asked what impacts he had witnessed of the enormous rise in population during his working lifetime. 'We monitor the vegetation. I've seen some changes.' His mind wandered to the coming season in the uplands, and he continued with excitement. 'It's amazing to see them in spring, and think about what they will eat. They love *Bistorta vivipara*; they dig out the roots. You can see holes where they've dug it. Later in the season they eat the leaves, then ptarmigan eat the seeds.'

Skarphéðinn's feelings for his Snæfell geese were plain. 'Geese mean a lot to me,' he said deliberately. 'They're one of my favourite birds. There was an election recently to choose our national favourite bird. The raven is likely to win, but it should be the pink-footed goose, I think.*

'But ravens are great birds too. They steal eggs from pink-footed geese. Did you know people harvest goose eggs here? They take thousands.' I asked whether this was legal. 'It is, as long as they leave two eggs in the nest.'

What were his personal highlights from his forty years with geese? 'Thinking back to the early days,' he said, 'one June, in a pink-footed goose's nest there was a lamb. The parent geese were fifty metres away, calling in distress. When the lamb got up, four goslings followed it! It was like something from Konrad Lorenz. The sheep are collected in

---

* In the end, Skarphéðinn later told me, the golden plover won.

the autumn, and taken to lowland corrals,' he continued. 'One farmer reported a full-grown goose following the sheep. It flew round and round the corral, looking for its adopted mother!

'Another time, I was living with a sheep farmer. It was in a valley close to Brú, near Anna's farm, where that British artist goes to paint.' So he too knew Jonathan Yule, who for thirty years has haunted the same bleak landscapes seeking geese. 'I was working in a hayfield in the summer. To my amazement, five or six pink-footed geese flew in and walked right up to us. We learned they had been raised on a farm nearby. They became our friends. Once I was riding on horseback and they were flying with me. I will never forget it. Then,' he broke off, 'in the autumn, they heard the call.'

But now it's spring again, or almost. 'Flocks are building in the hayfields,' he said. 'In three or four weeks they will be in the highlands, nesting.' The geese are home, I thought, my journey with them done.

I thanked Skarphéðinn for sharing his experience of geese in Iceland, and said goodbye. He cut me short: 'There's one more person you need to speak to. He was a farmer but he got involved with geese. Now he knows them better than anyone else. He's a sort of goose nerd.'

I smiled to think that in Iceland, as here in Norfolk, so many people loved the geese, and knew them: scientists, farmers, birdwatchers, photographers and hunters, all bound together in the story of these magnificent birds.

Friday 30th April

April has been bitter. All this month a cruel north wind has mocked us, stalling bird migration from the south,

April

cracking skin and earth, keeping people clothed in many layers. Spring's arrival – needed this year as never – has been grudging.

In front of me today, however, there are sacraments of spring. A pair of greylags picks across the short-mown, daisy-dappled grass beside the lake at Holkham Hall. The gander's legs are rhubarb pink; the goose's paler. Walking past, they stretch their necks, pointing vivid bills at me, flaring orange-outlined eyes. For at their feet are goslings, nine of them. The soft down of their days-old backs and crowns is silty brown; their bellies unsalted butter, warming gold in their cheeks and throats. Some of their rubbery bills are brown; some tipped in pink.

Beyond them, warier by far, stands a pair of barnacle geese. The gander has a broad black smudge between his bill and eye; the goose scarcely a pencilled line. Necks up, they are uneasy. Between them three little chicks – just two days old, I think – are tottering. The greylag chicks beside me are attractive, but these baby barnacles are Disneyed in their loveliness: dust grey above, fading to frost below. Their open faces have a primrose blush, marked only by their stubby bills, bright eyes and tiny skullcaps. I am entranced.

I was in a dark mind as I reached the park today. All winter, as I hurtled round North Norfolk on my old red bike, the roads were quiet; people and their cars locked down, at home. The tarmac, wet, miserable and muddy as it was, was mine. This morning the Dry Road was a hell of cars. Most took care to give me space; some tore by, only terrifying inches from me. Eleven miles I cycled north, angry and despairing at the world we have created, in which we're trapped, in which our cars and carbon melt the tundra needed by the geese, by biodiversity, and by ourselves. Even

The Meaning of Geese

the pearly apple blossom in the hedge, the yellowhammers and lesser whitethroats singing, could not rouse me from my mood. I'm frightened.

I meant to nurture this mean mood; to dwell in it, as I have for days. Here though, my bike laid on the grass behind me, goslings, and the new-hatched ducklings on the lake beyond them, have altered me. In the company of goslings it is hard to sulk. The adult barnacles are nervous, lowing gently to their little ones, wanting to keep them close. As a kite loops low above the water, one parent barks to bring them toddling back. Each time a dog walks by, though on a lead and twenty metres from the lake, they guide their fluffed flotilla onto water and swim away. These barnacles may be generations from their ancestors on Siberian, Svalbard or Greenland tundra, but their fear of Arctic foxes is unchanged.

I was amazed when Andy told me that a brood of barnacles had hatched already. Most of the Svalbard population of barnacle geese is on the Solway still, where more than 30,000 birds have been photographed this week. They are yet to travel north, to stake their territory on the tundra, mate, lay their eggs and incubate. Six weeks or more ahead of them, their Holkham cousins are hatching chicks; their behaviour changing rapidly as they adapt to life by a temperate lake. The more I've looked at geese this winter past, the more I've wondered; the more I've understood how much we have to learn about their shifting lives.

Next month Kane will come to Norfolk, to visit Holkham and Pensthorpe, with a view to ringing barnacles later in the summer. The founders of Pensthorpe's colony were captive escapes, some thirty years ago, but today's birds disappear in winter. The origin of Holkham's birds,

April

the first of which arrived just fifteen years ago, remains unknown. Perhaps Kane's Darvic rings, with which his team is fitting barnacle geese this year at colonies all over Wales and England, will start to tell their story: where they go in winter, how far they fly, whether they mix in winter with our Arctic flocks of pinkfeet and other geese. In just this way, since Scott and Fisher first visited Þjórsárver in summer 1951, rings, collars and geolocators have been unravelling the lives of geese.

Geese, and the people who live with them, have been my flock all winter. In August, just before the first geese came, fearful of dark months alone, with neither work nor family, I told myself I'd watch wild geese: get on my bike, get out, look, shiver, learn and write. I would not have made it through this Covid season but for them.

Now they have gone, taking their thrilling voices with them to the Arctic, their muscles primed with Norfolk sugar beet and grass. Some have formed lifetime pair bonds here this winter, and will try to breed this year. Some perished in late winter's heartless snow and some were shattered by gunshot: strong bodies turned in seconds into lifeless, tumbling weights, followed by piteous puffs of feathers. Some have gone north alone.

The space left in the landscape by the pinkfeet is filled by swallows now, by house martins purring over Holkham Hall, despite the unforgiving cold. Straining against the wind, a green-veined white is feeding in the sward beside me. A coot, his eyes like jasper beads, scurries across the lake, bearing an oak leaf to his female on her nest. I meant today to reach the saltmarsh, where some of Siberia's brent geese are gathered yet, waiting for days to lengthen further and for Taymyr to begin to thaw before they leave. I meant to bid them fortune

The Meaning of Geese

on their journey; to thank them for their winter company; to pray their tundra will persist a few years more, despite our ravaging of the climate. Here though, with these tiny goslings – their Arctic genes borne into another generation on Holkham's grass – my bike and I will stay.

Epilogue

Thirteen months later, in late May 2022, there are barnacle goslings in front of me again, at the south end of the lake in Holkham Park. The goslings – numbering 69 in 26 families – range from newly hatched, tottering on neat black feet, to month-olds, plump on Holkham's spring-sweet grass. The smallest families have just one gosling. The most successful pair has seven. I have come to count them and to read their parents' rings.

Kane and his ringing friends came to Norfolk several times last summer, to plan their catch of barnacle geese both at Holkham and at Pensthorpe. At five in the morning on 14th July, while most of the geese were in moult and flightless, a team of ringers, Holkham's wardens and gamekeepers and Wells wildfowlers gently walked the geese towards the lake. Once the birds were on the water, a flotilla of young canoeists appeared from behind an island cloaked in willows and guided them south along the lake towards the weir. The night before, a mesh fence had been stretched across the weir and a corral constructed in the shadow of a nearby beech, connected to the lake by a corridor of hurdles. Ringers and their helpers lined the banks as the canoeists herded the geese towards the weir. In a seething mass, the moulting geese trotted along the corridor into the safety of the corral. Kane and Andy's plan had been effected seamlessly.

The Meaning of Geese

The team ringed and measured 431 barnacle geese at Holkham, and 103 the following day at Pensthorpe, each with a metal ring from the British Trust for Ornithology on the right leg and a Darvic ring with a unique code on the left. Kane later told me how thrilled he was that so many people had come together to assist.

His chief thrill, though, was in the spectacle of these many geese by Holkham Hall, and in the anticipation of what they would teach us: 'There's something so exciting about releasing them with their markers, wondering what we will learn from them. I love that: finding out new things about a common species.'

In less than a year, these ringed Norfolk-nesting barnacle geese have taught us many things. Almost as soon as the geese left Holkham and Pensthorpe in August 2021, they began to be seen in coastal Suffolk. Geese from both sites were frequently seen together in Suffolk through the winter. In March and April 2022, as the geese returned to Norfolk, they were together still, with Holkham-ringed birds seen at Pensthorpe and Pensthorpe-ringed birds seen at Holkham too. It now seems very likely that the Holkham birds are satellites of the colony formed from captive barnacle geese at Pensthorpe in the 1980s.

What we have also learned, as Andy already suspected, is that the barnacle geese which winter on the grazing marshes of the Holkham National Nature Reserve – arriving in November and staying until February – are entirely separate from the birds which nest in the park. Over winter 2021–22 the hundreds of barnacles on the grazing marshes were all unringed. Where they come from we do not know, but we can be sure they are not from Holkham or from Pensthorpe.

Epilogue

Just like Peter Scott's Old Pink and the strange white-fronted pinkfoot which Mark, Stuart and I saw separately the winter before last, these ringed geese can now be recognised as individuals in the field. With this – though these remarkable birds have identities quite without our intervention – Holkham and Pensthorpe's barnacle geese now have stories understandable to human minds. And through the fathomless alchemy of the internet, these stories are readily accessible. Everyone who reads a ring and reports it to the project website receives the bird's life story and a map of the locations where it has been seen.

The two barnacle geese I'm watching now are ringed. The bigger, warier male of what is obviously a pair is K45; the female is F84. Three weeks after the catch, on 7th August 2021, I recorded them at Holkham as a pair, and saw that they had goslings, which were also ringed: H57 and H82. On 3rd November the adults and H57 were seen together in Southwold. Until today, nobody had seen them since.

There is one more tantalising detail to their story. F84 and K45 have not bred this year. While this year's breeding birds are with their fluffy goslings by the lake, between vibrant stands of yellow flag iris and reed sweet grass, the non-breeding birds have gathered in a larger flock behind the hall. F84 and K45 are among them. Though I know they failed to breed, trotting behind them is a little gosling. Yellowish below and mossy grey above, it is a greylag. Somehow F84 and K45 have adopted it or it has adopted them. As my dear friend Kell says of his beloved barnacles and greylags in the Netherlands, these resourceful birds surprise you endlessly.

I have read 85 goose rings today, all barnacles, except for ZX4, a greylag, also ringed last year. I have noted how many chicks are following each pair and which non-breeding geese

The Meaning of Geese

are paired, each observation adding minutely to our understanding of these lovely birds.

North of me, beyond the park, beyond the lake, the white-naped, speckle-headed chicks of lapwings scurry behind their burnished mothers in the grazing marsh, where in winter thousands of brents and pinkfeet graze. In a little more than three months, the first pinks will be here again, bringing winter in their wings. Just three weeks later, the first dark-bellied brents will come. And then the whitefronts. For another winter, they will bring the constant sunlight of the summer tundra to our edgeless Norfolk coast, and fill our fields and marshes with their Arctic clamour. For another winter we will watch, and paint, and shoot, and love them. For once you join the wild goose flocks, you're theirs.

For now, our Norfolk pinkfeet are with Hálfdán and with Skarphéðinn in Iceland: females nestled on their dull white eggs, and ganders standing watch nearby. Inside these down-cupped eggs, cells are dividing rapidly; carbon, minerals and energy from Norfolk's beet forged into Arctic life. Those few of this year's dusky goslings which grow to adulthood, which escape the jaws of Arctic foxes and skuas' cruel bills, will come south in the first days of September, bringing their shrill Norse gossip home to me.

But now it's summer. House martins huddle round a puddle by the lake beside me, gathering mud with which to build their nests. Nodding goodbye to K45, F84 and their changeling chick, I thank the geese for letting me flock with them all through a long, dark winter and I turn to summer sunshine and my home.

WILD GEESE, THEIR PEOPLE AND THEIR PLACES IN NORFOLK

Great flocks of wild geese can be found all around North Norfolk and the Broads in winter. They touch the lives of countless thousands of people. Listed here are some of the most important sites for them, the organisations which study and protect them, and the Norfolk artists who paint them, whose experience helped in the writing of this book.

Holkham

The Holkham Estate comprises perhaps the single most important site for geese in Norfolk and one of the most important in the UK. Tens of thousands of pink-footed geese visit the Holkham National Nature Reserve each winter, feeding across the surrounding arable landscape and roosting either on coastal mudflats or on freshwater lagoons. These flocks are joined every year by a handful of rarer geese.

The saltmarshes and grazing marshes of the Holkham NNR are also the winter home of many hundreds of dark-bellied brent geese, while a small flock of Russian white-fronted geese visits the grazing marshes too.

In recent years a growing colony of feral barnacle geese has nested by the lake in Holkham Park while a separate flock of barnacle geese (assumed to be of wild origin) has begun to winter on the grazing marshes.

It is Holkham's flocks which are the main characters in *The Meaning of Geese*.

holkham.co.uk

National Trust

The National Trust owns and manages large areas of North Norfolk saltmarsh and freshwater grazing marsh, which are internationally important for pink-footed and dark-bellied brent geese. National Trust nature reserves adjoin both the Holkham Estate and Norfolk Wildlife Trust Cley and Salthouse Marshes, to create a landscape which is protected for wild geese, biodiversity and the environment.

nationaltrust.org.uk

Norfolk Wildlife Trust

Norfolk Wildlife Trust was founded in 1926 to care for Cley Marshes, which had been purchased by twelve gentlemen friends as a reserve for birds. Ever since, Cley and Salthouse Marshes has been a wintering site for dark-bellied brent geese, which feed by day on the grazing marshes of the reserve and on surrounding arable land, and roost on Blakeney Pit by night. This flock is joined every year by a small number of pale-bellied brent geese and occasionally by a black brant. During the final stages of editing this book, in late winter and spring 2022, a stunning red-breasted goose visited the brent goose flock at Cley.

In the past few years several thousand pink-footed geese have roosted on the freshwater scrapes at Cley Marshes,

flying out to farmland across North Norfolk to feed. They are sometimes joined by Russian white-fronted geese and tundra bean geese.
norfolkwildlifetrust.org.uk

RSPB

Since 1889, the RSPB has acted on behalf of wild birds and their habitats, in the UK and across the world.

In Norfolk, thousands of pink-footed geese roost on the mudflats off the RSPB reserve at Snettisham, while thousands of dark-bellied brent geese use the saltmarshes and grazing marshes which stretch from Snettisham east to RSPB Titchwell Marsh.

In the Norfolk Broads, RSPB Buckenham Marshes supports a winter flock of Russian white-fronted geese, while in recent years it has also held a winter flock of several thousand pink-footed geese. The reserve has traditionally been one of two UK winter sites for the elegant taiga bean goose, though this flock has dwindled almost to the point of disappearance, most likely as a result of climate change.
rspb.org.uk

Waterbird Colour-marking Group

The feral barnacle geese which nest around the lake in Holkham Park, and those which nest at Pensthorpe, have been colour-ringed, under licence from the British Trust for Ornithology, by the Waterbird Colour-marking Group. Sightings can be submitted to their website. Observers receive a life history of the birds they have seen.
waterbirdcolourmarking.org

Wildfowl and Wetlands Trust

The brainchild of Sir Peter Scott, The Wildfowl and Wetlands Trust has grown to become a global force for the study and conservation of wetlands and the organisms which inhabit them.

Though WWT's Norfolk reserve at Welney is most celebrated for its winter swans, other reserves across the UK are of international importance for geese. They include Caerlaverock on the Solway Firth, which is winter home to thousands of barnacle geese from Svalbard, and Martin Mere in Lancashire, which supports pink-footed geese from autumn to spring. WWT's original reserve, at Slimbridge in Gloucestershire, is visited each winter by a flock of Russian white-fronted geese.
wwt.org.uk

James McCallum

A native of the port town of Wells, James McCallum is the most celebrated wild-goose artist of his generation, spending every winter painting North Norfolk's flocks of pinkfeet and brents. His paintings draw on a lifetime spent watching geese with an exceptional eye for their plumage, movement and behaviour.
jamesmccallum.co.uk

Jonathan Yule

For decades, since an inspiring encounter with Peter Scott, artist Jonathan Yule has painted the wild landscapes of Norfolk and their geese. For almost as long, he has made annual pilgrimages to eastern Iceland to watch and paint pink-footed geese on their upland breeding grounds.
jonathanyule.com

ACKNOWLEDGEMENTS

This book would not exist without the knowledge, skill, encouragement and generosity of countless friends and colleagues.

Four people stand out for the huge amount they contributed. For boundless information, critical reading, companionship and unstinting encouragement, I extend my profound thanks to Andy Bloomfield, Kane Brides and James McCallum. They are true goose experts and without them this story would have little merit. My fourth unwavering ally has been my editor, Muna Reyal of Chelsea Green, whose humour, diligence and creative insight have improved my writing and storytelling at every turn.

Many others were my companions, readers, teachers, fixers, guides and friends through the preparation of this book and to all of them I am deeply indebted. They are (in alphabetical order by family name): George Acheson, Anne Balfour, Ashley and Claudia Banwell, Lee Barber, Patrick Barkham, Joe Beckham, Twiggy Bigwood, Javier Caletrío, Tom Cameron, Dominic Castle, Sujan Chatterjee, Professor Andy Clarke, Louise Clewley, Anna Cowie, Andrew and Sheelin Cuthbert, Stuart Darbyshire, Natalie Douglas, Gary Elton, Kell and Alison Eradus, Jake Fiennes, Jonnie Fisk, Dave and Caroline Gittens, Mark Golley and Lynnette Nicholson, Tess Handby, Mike Harmer, Melissa Harrison, David and Sue Hayes, Martin Hayward Smith, Hálfdán Helgi Helgason, Dave and Bizz Horsley, Gav Horsley, Rich

Hoyer, Kit Jewitt, Gayatri Kaul, Chrissie Kelley, Jerry Kinsley, Ben Lewis, James Lowen, David Lyles, Rebecca Lyon, Kat MacPherson, Aimee McIntosh, Harriet Mead, Tim Melling, Harry Mitchell, David North, Robin and Helen Owen, Professor Debbie Pain, Nick Parsons, Lin Pateman, Sue Penlington, Professor Jeff Price, Hazel Ratcliffe, Ashley Saunders, Dafila Scott, Cameron Self, Rob Smith, Tim Stowe, Brigit Strawbridge Howard, David Stubbs and Jan Mata, Kevin Thatcher, Skarphéðinn Þórisson, Berend Voslamber and Jonathan Yule.

The binoculars and telescope which I used throughout my goose-watching winter, and which I have used for years, have kindly been lent to me by my friends at Viking Optical. My old red bike was serviced and repaired by R. J. Francis of Fakenham.

To anyone who helped me while I was writing this book, whom I have inadvertently neglected to thank, I extend my apologies and my thanks. Your contribution was no less valued.

My final thanks to Norfolk's wild geese, for letting me flock with them through a long cold winter, and throughout my life.

BIBLIOGRAPHY

Hudson, W. H. *Adventures Among Birds*. London: Dent, 1935.

Kear, Janet. *Man and Wildfowl*. London: Bloomsbury Publishing (UK) Poyser, 1990.

Lockwood, W. B. *The Oxford Book of British Bird Names*. Oxford: Oxford University Press, 1984.

McCallum, James. *Wild Goose Winter: Observations of Geese in North Norfolk*. Wells-next-the-Sea: Silver Brant, 2001.

Rutt, Stephen. *Wintering: A Season with Geese*. London: Elliott & Thompson, 2020.

Scott, Peter. *Morning Flight*. London: Country Life Limited, 1935.

Scott, Peter. *The Eye of the Wind*. London: Hodder & Stoughton, 1977.

Scott, Peter, and Hugh Boyd. *Wildfowl of the British Isles*. London: Country Life Limited, 1957.

Scott, Peter, and James Fisher. *A Thousand Geese*. Boston: Houghton Mifflin, 1954.

Stevenson, Henry, and Thomas Southwell. *The Birds of Norfolk, with Remarks on Their Habits, Migration and Local Distribution*. 3 Vol. London, 1866.

Taylor, Moss, Michael Seago, Peter Allard and Don Dorling. *Birds of Norfolk*. London: Pica Press, 1999.

White, T. H. *The Book of Merlyn*. London: Flamingo, 1977.

Yule, Jonathan. *Under a Colour-Washed Sky: From Norfolk Marshes to Icelandic Mountains*. Norfolk: Mascot Media, 2019.

ABOUT THE AUTHOR

Nick Acheson grew up in North Norfolk, where generations of his family on both sides have lived and farmed. Since early childhood he has been fascinated by nature, a fascination which grew through his youth to become a consuming interest and a commitment to wildlife conservation. In adulthood this has developed into advocacy for the environment and for a sustainable future.

Following his degrees, Nick volunteered for three months on an ornithological research project in lowland Bolivia. He came home after ten years, having worked the length and breadth of the country, and further afield across South America: in nature conservation and with indigenous communities in sustainable development.

For the past fifteen years, Nick has worked for conservation NGOs in the UK, notably Norfolk Wildlife Trust. He is an ambassador for both Norfolk Wildlife Trust and Pensthorpe, a trustee of Felbeck Trust and a recent president of the historic Norfolk and Norwich Naturalists' Society. He is well known as a speaker, teacher and contributor to the media on nature and conservation.

Nick has written columns in the *Norfolk Magazine* and in Norfolk Wildlife Trust's *Tern* magazine for several years and is editor of the latter. He has written for three of the *Seasons* anthologies (Elliot and Thompson), *Red Sixty Seven* (British Trust for Ornithology), *Low-Carbon Birding* (Pelagic Publishing), *British Birds*, *British Wildlife* and *BBC Wildlife*. This is his first book.